PIANO • VOCAL • GUITAR

INTEGRITY
MODERN WORSHIP
ANTHOLOGY

ISBN 978-1-4584-0014-7

HAL•LEONARD® CORPORATION
7777 W. BLUEMOUND RD. P.O. BOX 13819 MILWAUKEE, WI 53213

For all works contained herein:
Unauthorized copying, arranging, adapting, recording, Internet posting, public performance,
or other distribution of the printed music in this publication is an infringement of copyright.
Infringers are liable under the law.

Visit Hal Leonard Online at
www.halleonard.com

CONTENTS

4	All to You
11	Amazed
16	At the Foot of the Cross
20	Be Still and Know
25	Come Thou Fount, Come Thou King
30	Counting on God
36	Everlasting God
42	Filled with Glory
48	Glorified
58	God You Reign
64	A Greater Song
53	Hear Us from Heaven
70	Here in Your Presence
76	Holy God
82	Hosanna (Praise Is Rising)
90	How He Loves
106	I Am Free
114	I Need You More
97	I Will Boast
118	Just to Be with You
124	Let the Praises Ring
132	Lord Have Mercy
136	Love the Lord
144	Mercy
152	The More I Seek You

158	Moving Forward
166	My Savior Lives
172	New Doxology
176	A New Hallelujah
183	Open Up the Sky
190	Our God Saves
204	Overcome
197	Promises
212	Ready Now
220	Revelation Song
226	Rising
233	Stay Amazed
238	Thank You, Lord
245	Today (As for Me and My House)
252	Today Is the Day
260	What Can I Do?
266	Worshiping You
271	You Are for Me
278	You Are God Alone (not a god)
292	You Are Good
287	You Are the One
298	You Gave Your Life Away
314	Your Great Name
305	Your Love Never Fails
322	Your Name

ALL TO YOU

Words and Music by LINCOLN BREWSTER
and REID McNULTY

no, ___ no.
no, ___ no. I've searched __ and __ came up emp-ty; this world has noth-ing for __ me. __

You are my one __ and on - ly. __

I'm liv-ing __ my __ life for __ You, __

E
B
C♯m7
A
4fr
and I'm giv - ing ev - 'ry - thing to You.
E
B/D♯
C♯m7
B
A
Not hold - ing back, but ev - 'ry part, I'm
1
F♯m7
E
B
C♯m7
A
giv-ing it all to You.
E
B
C♯m7
A
2
F♯m7
giv-ing it all to You.

I'm living my life for You, and I'm giving ev-'ry-thing to You. Not hold-ing back, but ev-'ry part, I'm giv-ing it all to You.

I'm giv-ing it all.

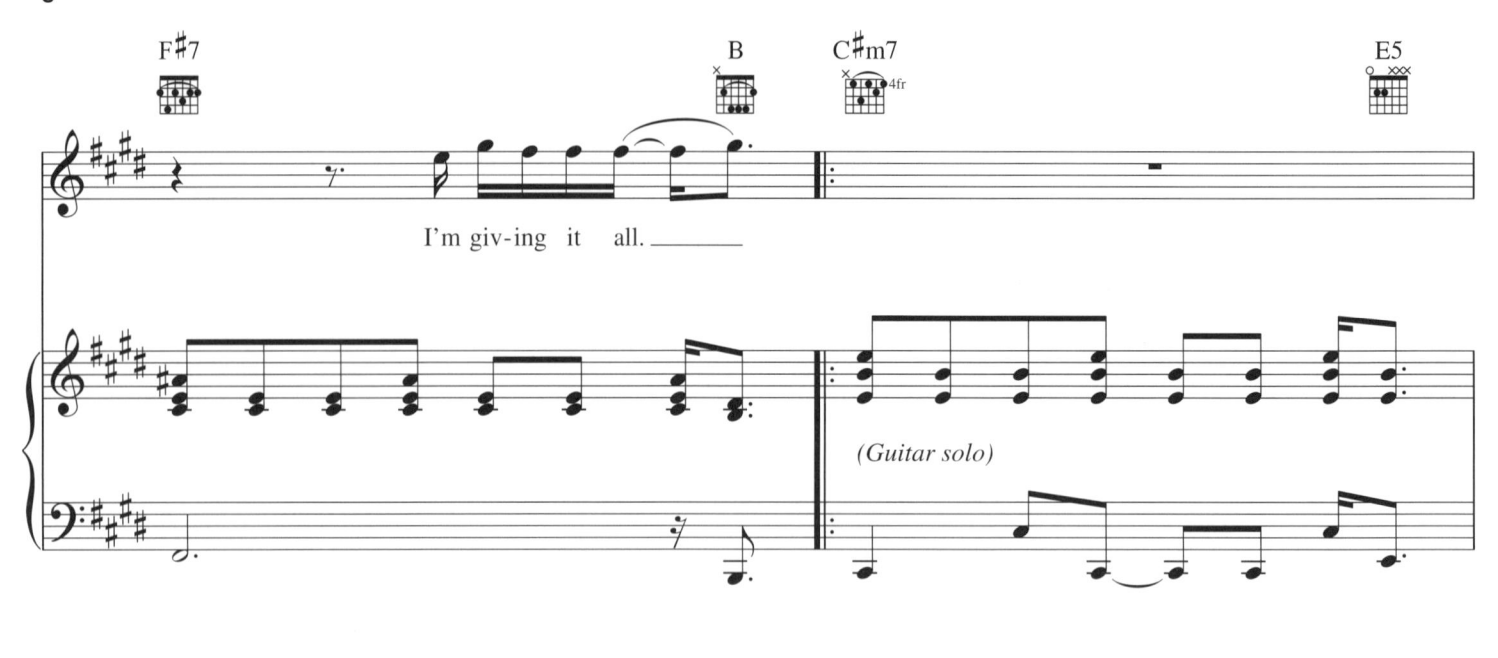

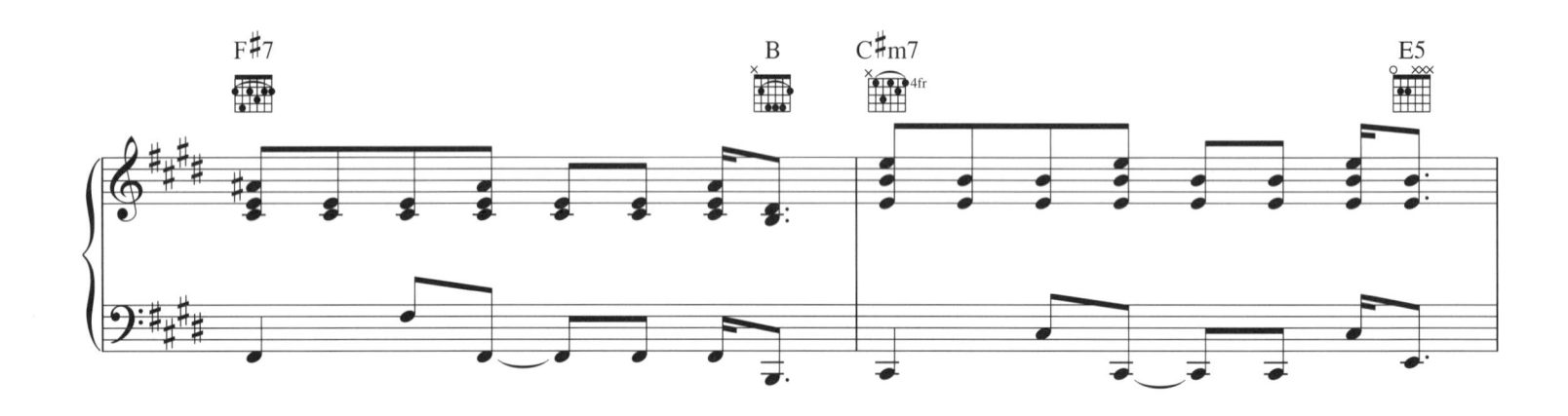

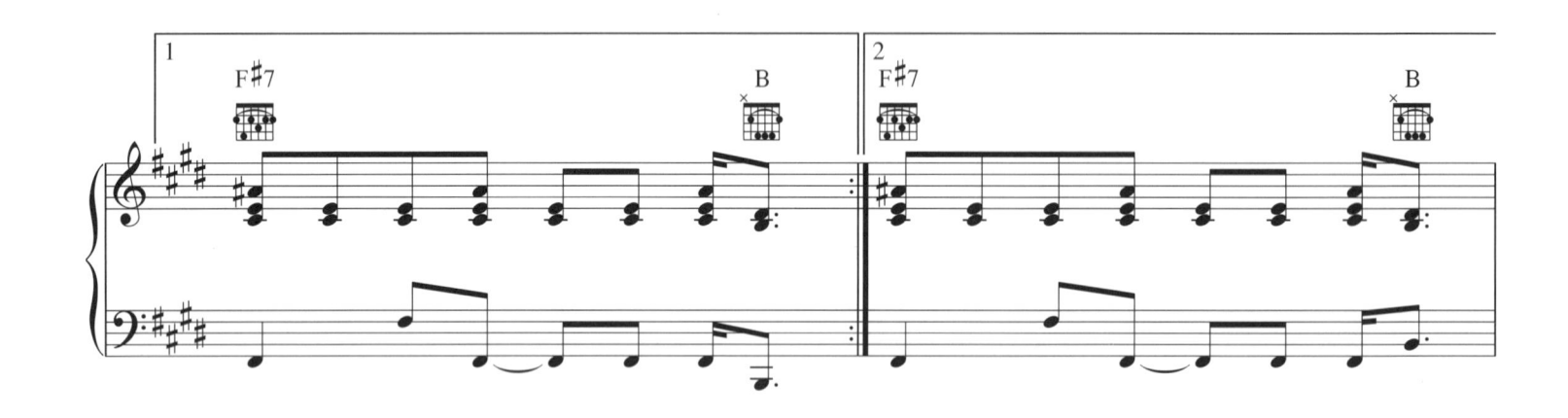

(Guitar solo)

I'm living my life for You, and I'm giving ev'ry-thing to You. Not holding back, but ev'ry part, I'm giving it all to You.

CODA
giving it all to You.

I'm giv-ing it all to You.
(Vocal ad lib. on repeat)

I'm giv-ing it all to You.

I'm giv-ing it all to You.

Whoa, oh.

AMAZED

Words and Music by
JARED ANDERSON

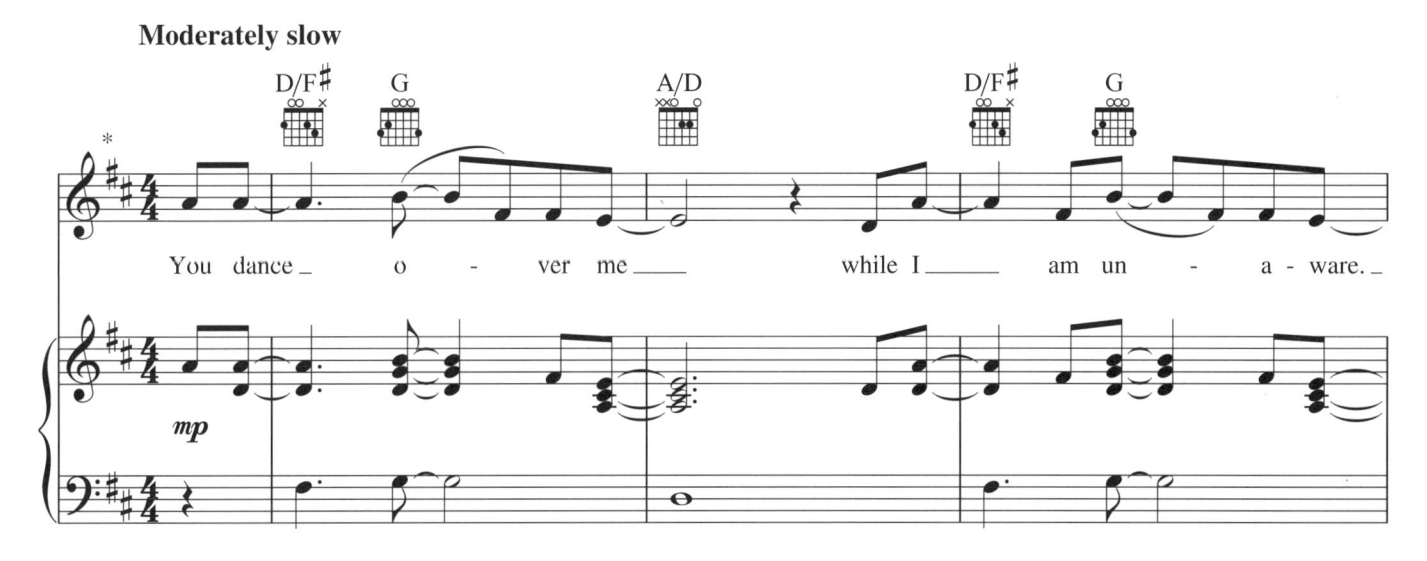

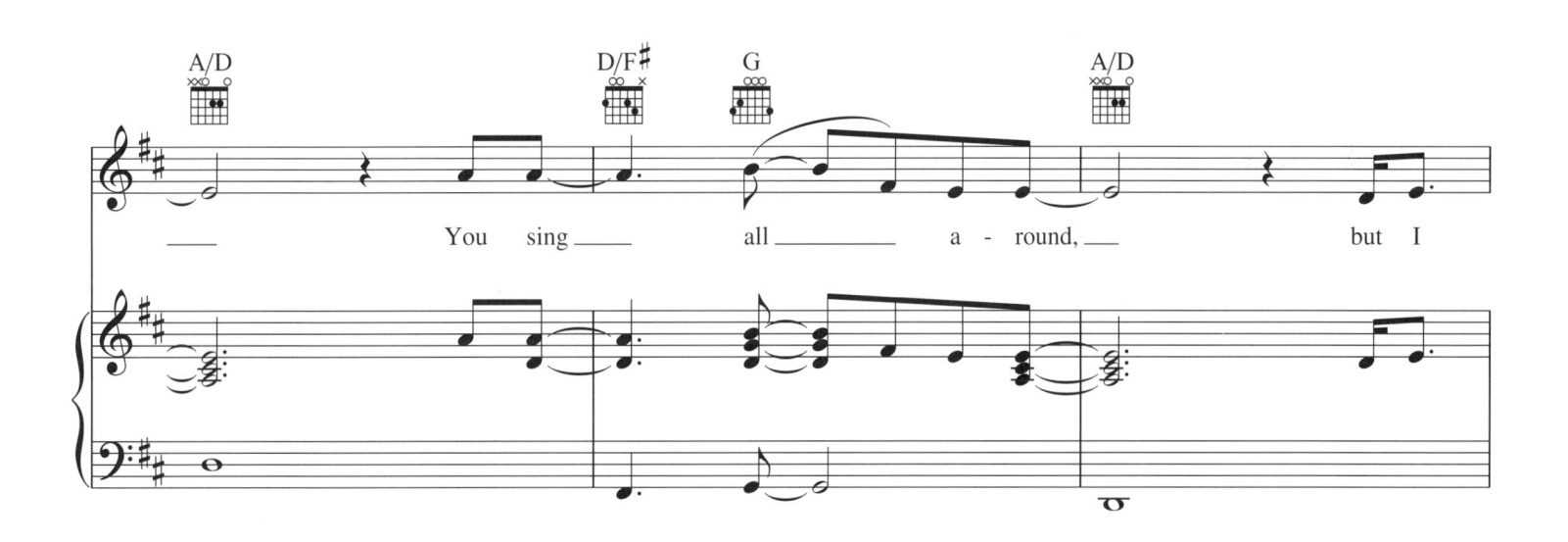

Moderately slow

You dance over me while I am unaware. You sing all around, but I never hear the sound. Lord, I'm amazed by You.

*Recorded a half step lower.

© 2003 VERTICAL WORSHIP SONGS (ASCAP)
Admin. at EMICMGPUBLISHING.COM
All Rights Reserved Used by Permission

12

A/D D/F♯ G A
You hold me in Your hand. Lord, I'm a - mazed
G(add2) A F♯m7
by You. Lord, I'm a - mazed by You.
G Em7 A
Lord, I'm a - mazed by You, how You love
D
me. How wide,

how deep,

how great is Your love for me.

How wide, is Your love for me.

And Lord, I'm amazed

G(add2)
A
F♯m7
by You. Lord, I'm a - mazed by You.
f
G
Em7
Lord, I'm a - mazed by You,
1
A
D
how You love me. Oh,
Lord, I'm a - mazed
2
A
D
how You love me.

AT THE FOOT OF THE CROSS

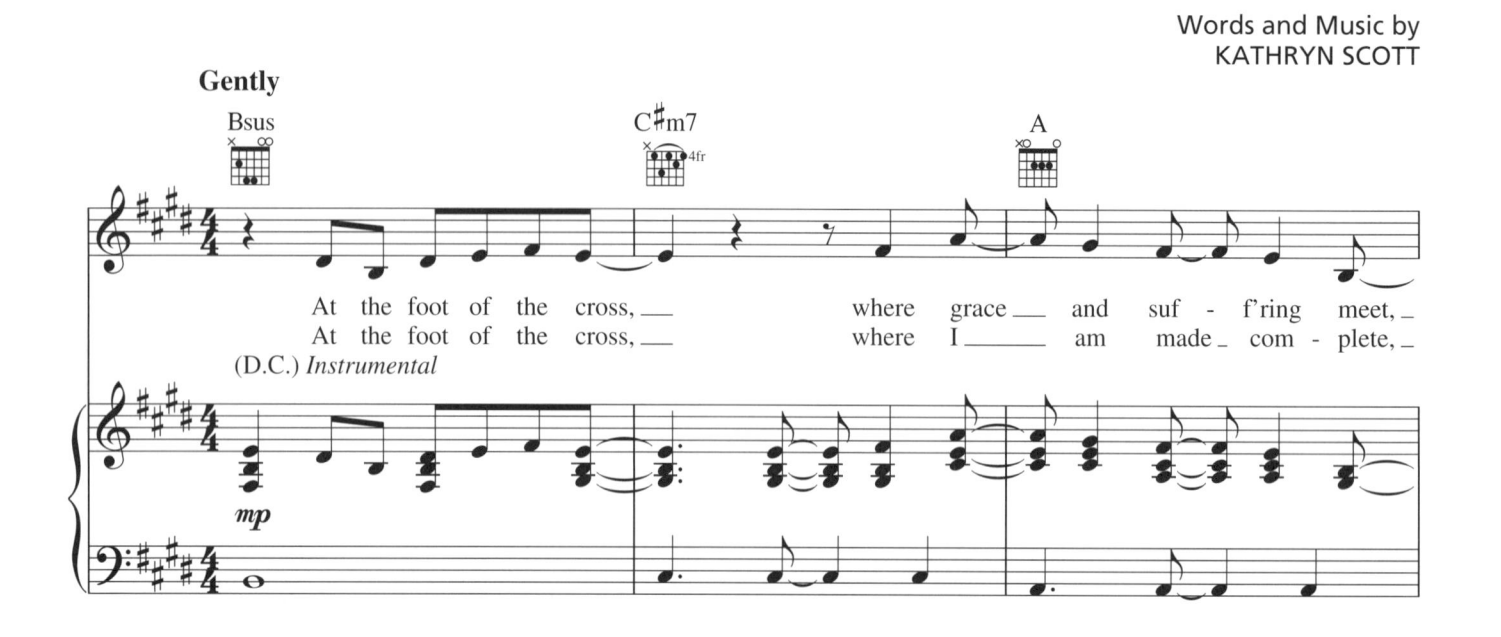

Words and Music by
KATHRYN SCOTT

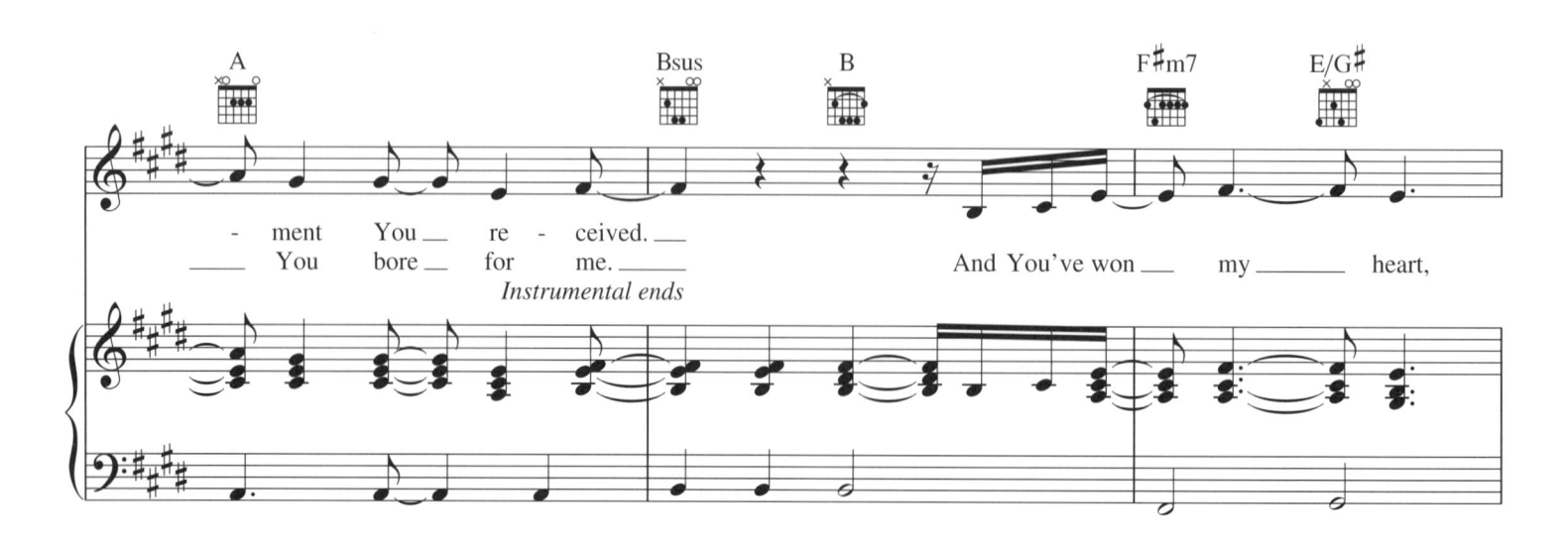

Gently

At the foot of the cross, where grace and suff'ring meet,
At the foot of the cross, where I am made complete,

(D.C.) Instrumental

You have shown me Your love through the judg-
You have given me life through the death

-ment You re-ceived.
You bore for me.
Instrumental ends

And You've won my heart,

© 2003 VERTICAL WORSHIP SONGS (ASCAP)
Admin. at EMICMGPUBLISHING.COM
All Rights Reserved Used by Permission

yes, You've won my heart. Now I can trade these ash-es in for beau-ty and wear for-give-ness like a crown. Com-ing to kiss the feet of mer-cy, I lay ev-'ry bur-den down at the foot of the cross.

2, 3
F♯m7
B
E
B
at the foot of the cross. I trade these ash - es in for
F♯m7
E
B
beau - ty and wear for - give - ness like a crown.
F♯m7
E
B
F♯m7
Com - ing to kiss the feet of mer - cy, I lay
To Coda
C♯m
4fr
B
F♯m7
B
E
D.C. al Coda
(take 2nd ending)
ev - 'ry bur - den down at the foot of the cross.

19

BE STILL AND KNOW

Words and Music by NANCY GORDON and STEVE MERKEL

Slowly and gently

mp

With pedal

still__ and know__ that I__ am__ God.__ Be

© 2006 INTEGRITY'S HOSANNA! MUSIC (ASCAP)
Admin. at EMICMGPUBLISHING.COM
All Rights Reserved   Used by Permission

C
G/B
Am7
G/B
still and know that I am God. Be
Am
G
F
still and know that I am God. Be
To Coda
Am
G
F
still and know that I am God.
C
G/B
Am7
G/B

C G/B Am7 G/B
Am G F C/E
God is our ref - uge and strength,
Am F Dm7
a ver - y pres - ent help in trou - ble.
G C G/B
Be still and know that I am

Am7 G/B C G/B
God. Be still and know that I am
Am7 G/B Am G
God. There-fore, we will not fear, e-ven
F C/E Am F
though the earth be re-moved and all the moun-tains be car-

-ried in-to ____ the midst of the sea. ____ Be-

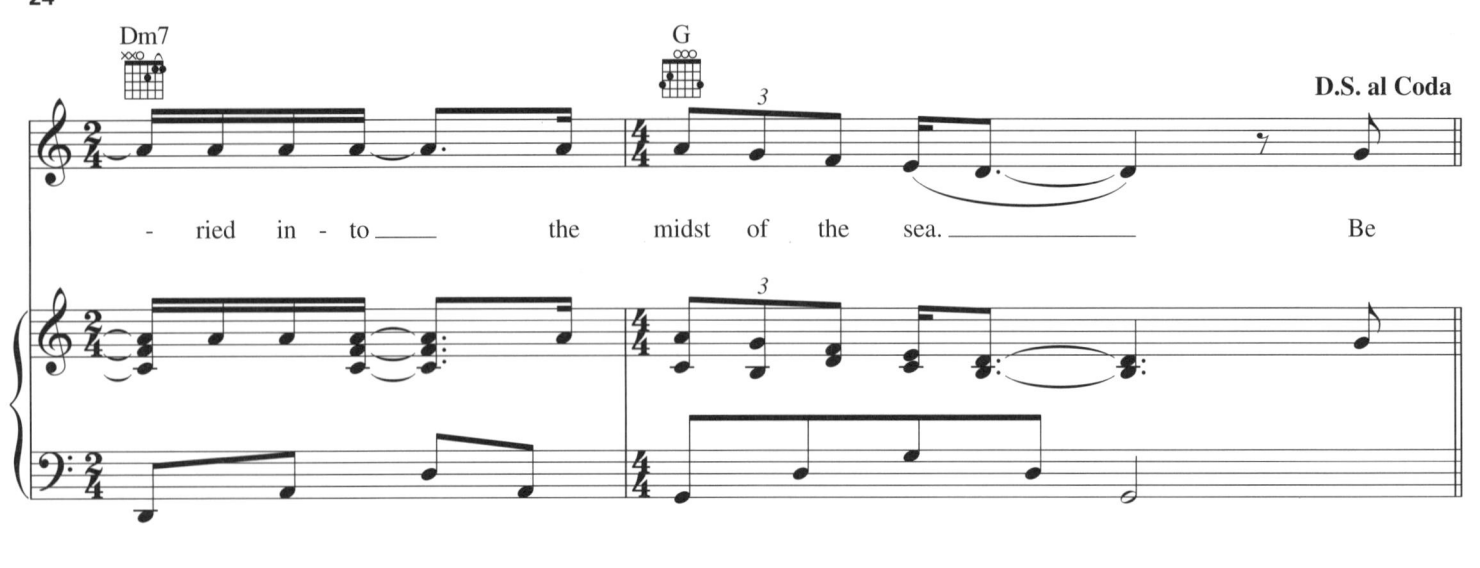

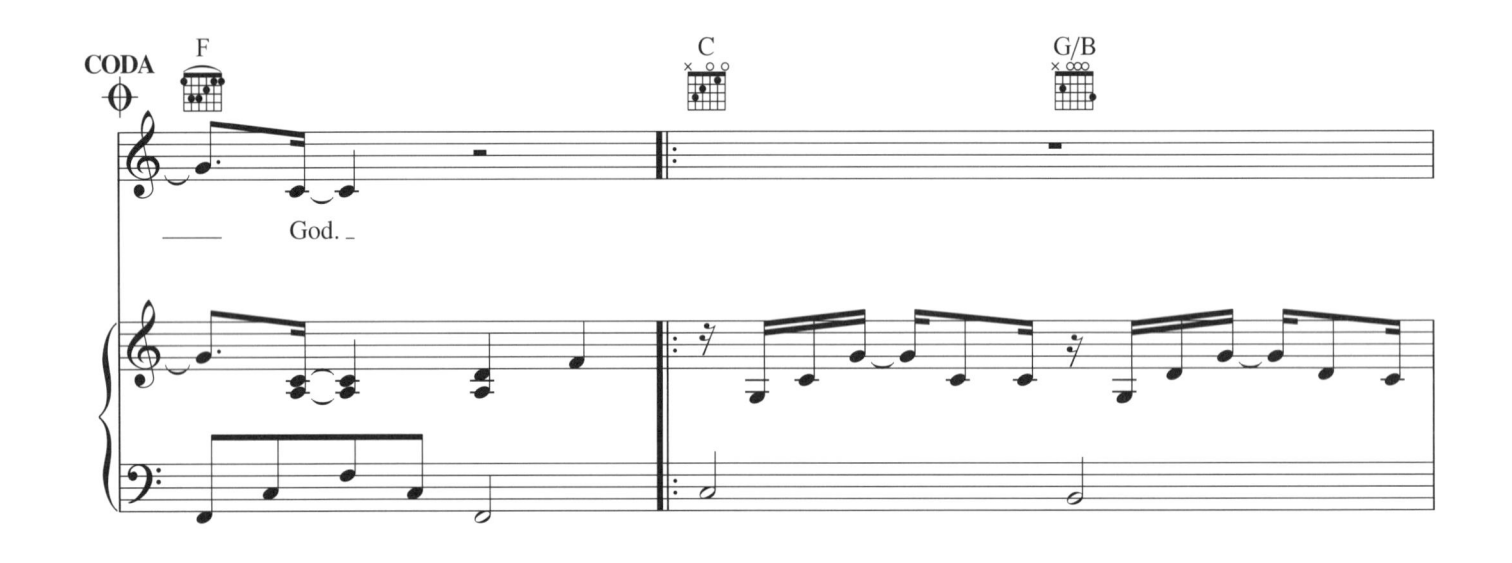

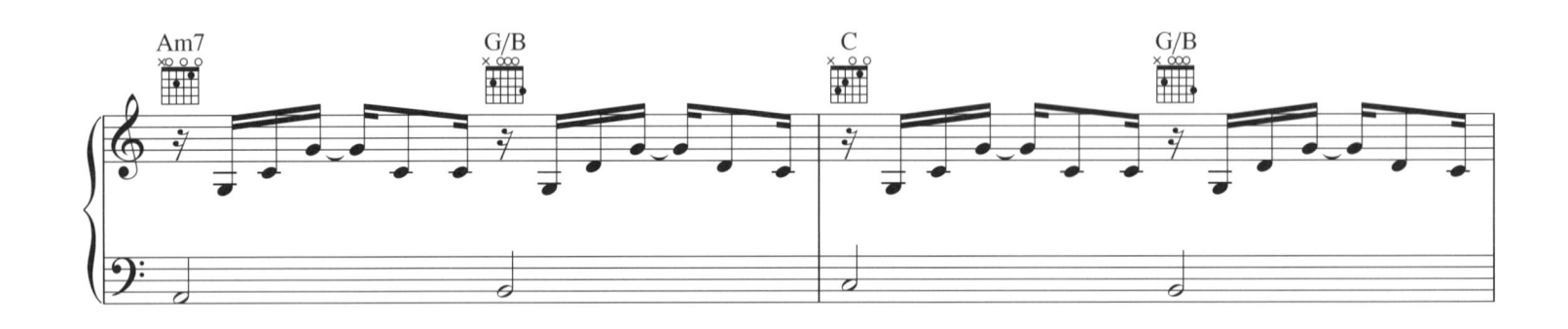

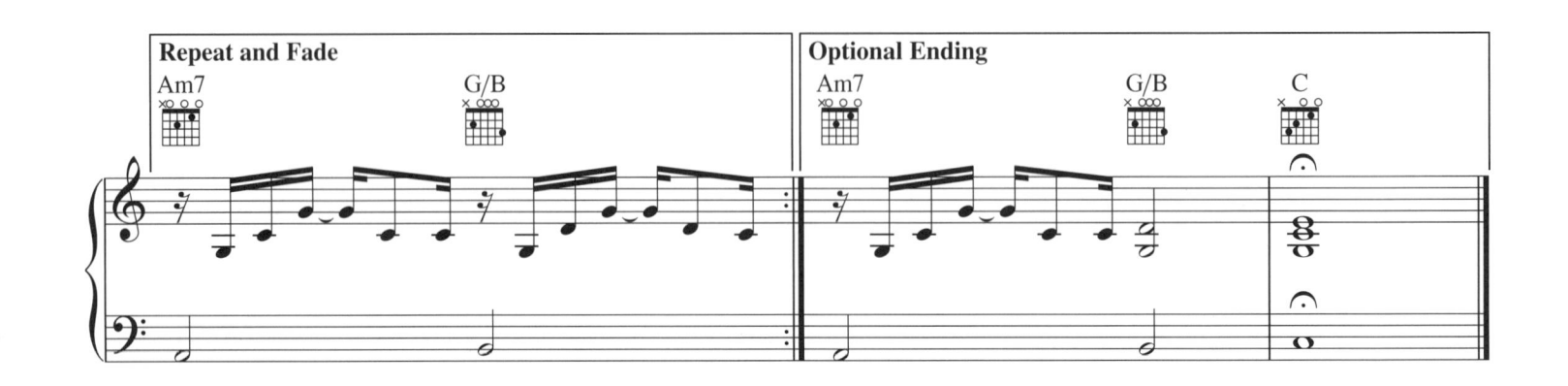

God. __

COME THOU FOUNT, COME THOU KING

Traditional
Additional Words and Music by
THOMAS MILLER

With movement

Come Thou Fount of ev-'ry bless-ing, tune my heart to sing Thy grace. Streams of mercy, nev-er ceas-ing, call for songs of loud-est

lost in ut-ter dark-ness till You came and res-cued me. I was bound by all my sin when Your love came and set me

grace, how great a debt-or dai-ly I'm con-strained to be. Let Thy good-ness, like a fet-ter, bind my wan-d'ring heart to

© 2005 GATEWAY CREATE PUBLISHING (BMI)
Admin. at EMICMGPUBLISHING.COM
All Rights Reserved   Used by Permission

praise. Teach me some melodious sonnet sung by
free. Now my soul can sing a new song, now my
Thee. Prone to wander, Lord, I feel it, prone to

flaming tongues above. Praise the mount, I'm fixed up-
heart has found a home. Now Your grace is always
leave the God I love. Here's my heart, Lord, take and

on it, mount of Thy redeeming love.
with me, and I'll
seal it, and seal it

I was

never be a-lone. Come Thou Fount, come Thou King, come Thou pre-cious Prince of Peace. Hear Your bride, to You we sing: Come Thou Fount of all bless-ing. Come Thou ing.

D.S. al Coda
D/F♯ A5/E D/F♯ Gsus2 D/F♯ A5/E D Dsus2
O to
CODA
G/B A/C♯ D Dsus2 D Dsus2 D
for Thy courts a - bove.
Vocal ad lib. on repeats
Dsus D Dsus2
1-3
D
4
D
Come Thou
G D/F♯ G
Fount, come Thou King, come Thou pre - cious Prince of

D/F♯
Bm
D/F♯
G(add2)
Peace. Hear Your bride, to You we sing: Come Thou
D/A
A
1
D
2
D
A5/E
Fount of all bless - ing. Come Thou ing.
D/F♯
A5/E
D/F♯
Gsus2
D/F♯
A5/E
D
D/F♯
A5/E
D
A5/E
D/F♯
A5/E
D/F♯
Gsus2
D/F♯
A5/E
D5
5fr

COUNTING ON GOD

Words and Music by
JARED ANDERSON

Up-tempo Rock

*Recorded a half step lower.

© 2007 VERTICAL WORSHIP SONGS (ASCAP)
Admin. at EMICMGPUBLISHING.COM
All Rights Reserved Used by Permission

_____ that's Yours. _____ Joy un-speak-a-ble that won't go a-way, _____ and just _____ e-nough strength to live for to-day. _____ So I nev-er have to wor-ry what to-mor-row will bring, _____ 'cause my faith _____ is on sol-id rock.

I am count-ing on God. I am count-ing on, I am count-ing on God.

32

| Am | G | C |

I am count-ing on, I am count-ing on God. I am count-ing on,

| F | Am | 1. G | To Coda ⊕

I am count-ing on God. I am count-ing on, I am count-ing on God.

| C | F | Am | G |

| C | F | Am | G |

I'm in a

I am count-ing on God.

And the mir-a-cle of Christ in me is the mys-ter-y that sets me free.

I'm nothing like I used to be, just open up your eyes, you'll see. Joy unspeakable that won't go away, and just enough strength to live for today. So I never have to worry what tomorrow will bring, 'cause my faith is on solid rock.

I am count-ing on God. I am count-ing on, I am count-ing on God.

I am count-ing on, I am count-ing on God. I am count-ing on,

I am count-ing on God. I am count-ing on, I am count-ing on God.

D.S. al Coda

CODA

I am count-ing on God.

rit.

EVERLASTING GOD

Words and Music by
GLENN PACKIAM

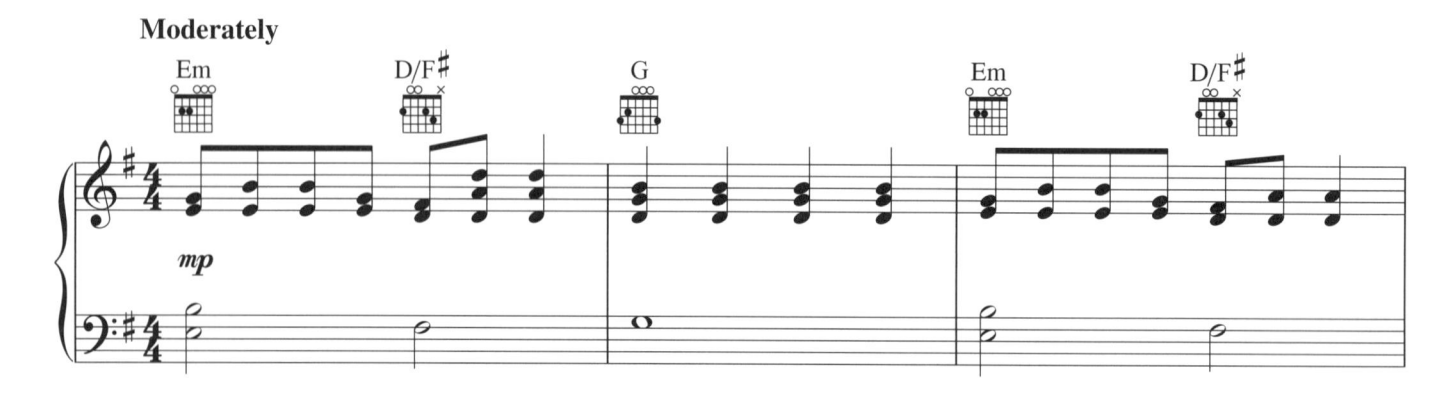

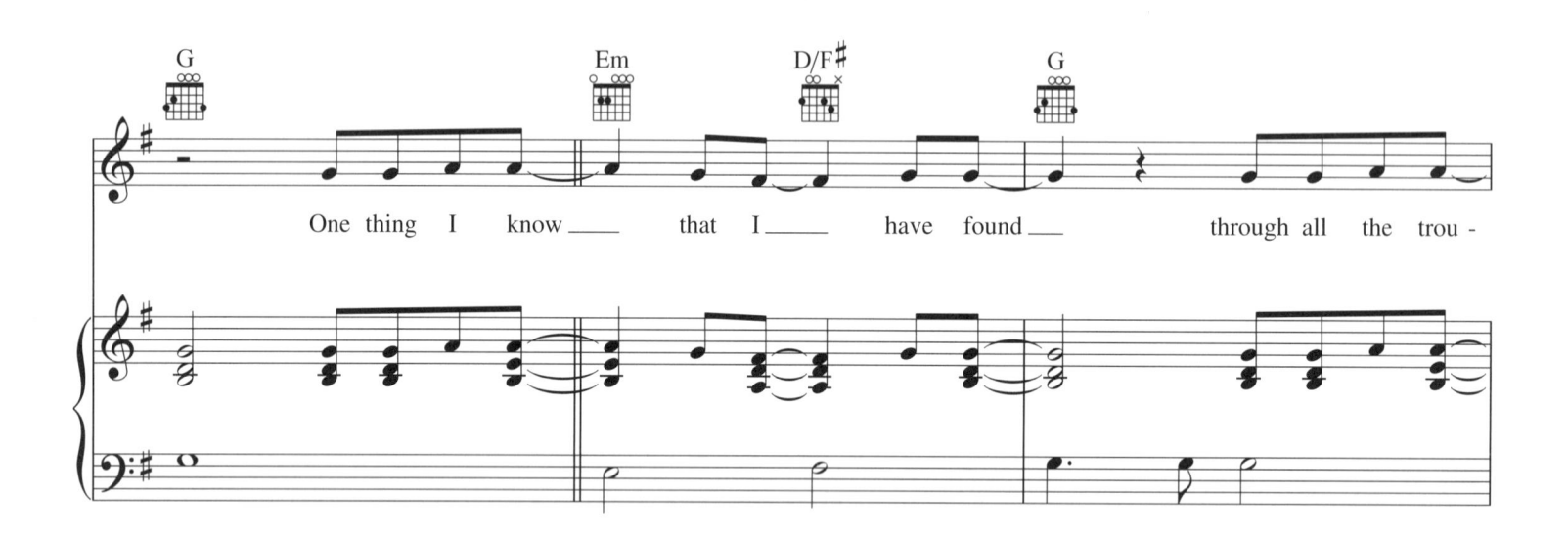

Moderately

One thing I know ___ that I ___ have found ___ through all the trou-bles that ___ sur- round. ___ You are the Rock ___ that nev- er fails, ___

© 2006 VERTICAL WORSHIP SONGS (ASCAP)
Admin. at EMICMGPUBLISHING.COM
All Rights Reserved   Used by Permission

37

| Cmaj7 | Am7 | D |

You nev-er fail. One thing I know

| Em | D/F# | G |

that I be-lieve through ev-'ry bless-
that I have found through all the trou-

| Em | D/F# | G |

-ing I re-ceive. You are the on-
-bles that sur-round. You are the Rock

| Em | D | Cmaj7 |

-ly one that stays, You al-ways stay.
that nev-er fails, You nev-er fail.

Am7
D
Csus2
3fr
You nev - er change,
You're still the same,
mf
G/B
C/E
D/F♯
G
You are the ev - er - last - ing God.
You will re - main
Csus2
3fr
G/B
C/E
D/F♯
af - ter the day has gone and things of earth have passed.
To Coda
G/B
Csus2
3fr
D
Em
D/F♯
Ev - er - last - ing God.

39

Ev-er-last-ing, ev-er-last-ing, ev-er-last-ing God.

Yeah.

You nev-er change, You're still the same,

You are the ev-er-last-ing God. You will re-main

after the day has gone and things of earth have passed.

Ev - er - last - ing God.

Ev - er - last - ing God. Yeah.

FILLED WITH GLORY

Words and Music by MICHAEL GUNGOR
and LISA GUNGOR

With praise and awe

As we all bow down, as we all come casting off our crowns, would You hear our cry? We want to see You glorified.

© 2005 VERTICAL WORSHIP SONGS (ASCAP) and LISA GUNGOR MUSIC
VERTICAL WORSHIP SONGS Admin. at EMICMGPUBLISHING.COM
All Rights Reserved   Used by Permission

As we __ Glo-ri-fy Your name, __ glo-ri-fy Your name, __ glo-ri-fy Your name. __ We want to see __ You glo-ri-fied. __

A♭ E♭ A♭/E♭ E♭
As I join as one, as we live
E♭/G A♭ B♭sus E♭/G A♭
to let Your king - dom come, Fa - ther, through our lives
Cm7 A♭ B♭sus E♭
we want to see You glo - ri - fied. Glo - ri -
A♭ B♭sus E♭ A♭ B♭
fy Your name, glo - ri - fy Your name,

45

filled with glo - ry. The earth will be filled with glo - ry, *like wa - ter o'er the sea,__ filled with glo - ry. The earth will be filled with glo - ry, like wa - ter o'er the sea.__ Glo - ri - fy Your name,__ glo - ri - fy Your name,__*

E♭maj7/G
A♭
B♭
Cm7
glo - ri - fy Your name.
We want to see
A♭
B♭sus
1
E♭/G
2
E♭
You glo - ri - fied.
Glo - ri -
We want to see
A♭
B♭sus
E♭
A♭
You glo - ri - fied.
E♭
A♭
E♭(add2)
4fr
3fr
6fr

GLORIFIED

Words and Music by
JARED ANDERSON

Praise belongs to You; let ev-'ry king-dom bow,
Praise belongs to You; let songs of chil-dren rise.

let ev-'ry o-cean roar, let ev-'ry heart a-dore You now.
You si-lence all Your foes, You set Your glo-ry in the skies.

© 2008 VERTICAL WORSHIP SONGS (ASCAP)
Admin. at EMICMGPUBLISHING.COM
All Rights Reserved   Used by Permission

Praise be-longs to You; what can I do but sing? The great-est joy I've found
Praise be-longs to You; cre-a-tion's call-ing now for the King to be re-vealed.
is to lay a crown be-fore my King, be-fore my King.
O King of Heav-en, come down. King of Heav - en, come
down.
I've come to wor - ship,
I've come to lift up Your name, for You de-serve this life laid down like the one that You gave.

I have but one voice, one heart and one sac-ri-fice, so would You take this life laid down and be glo-ri-fied, be glo-ri-fied.

Be glo-ri-fied, be glo-ri-fied.

51

Be glo-ri-fied, ____ Be glo-ri-fied.

I've come to wor-ship, I've come to lift up Your name, for You de-serve this life laid down like the one that You gave. I have but one voice, one heart and one sac-ri-fice, so would You take this life laid down and be glo-ri-fied. ____

HEAR US FROM HEAVEN

Words and Music by
JARED ANDERSON

Moderately

Lord, hear our cry, come heal our land.
Lord, hear our prayer, forgive our sins.

Breathe life into these dry and thirsty souls.
As we call on Your name, would You make this a place

---

* Recorded a half step higher.

© 2004 VERTICAL WORSHIP SONGS (ASCAP)
Admin. at EMICMGPUBLISHING.COM
All Rights Reserved   Used by Permission

for Your glo - ry to dwell?__ O - pen the blind__ eyes, un - lock the deaf__ ears, come to Your peo - ple as we draw near.__ Hear us from heav - en, touch our gen - er - a - tion. We are Your peo - ple, cry - ing out__ in des - per - a - tion.__

Lord, hear our song, Your children worship. As we sing out Your praise, would You make this a place for Your glory to dwell? Open the blind eyes, unlock the deaf ears, come to Your people as we draw near. Hear us from heav-

-en, touch our gen-er-a - tion. We are Your peo - ple, cry-ing out__ in des - per - a - tion.__

Hear us from heav - en, hear us from heav - en, hear us from heav-

Am
Fmaj7
G
C
- en. O - pen the blind eyes, un - lock the deaf
C/B
Dm7
Fmaj7
G
ears, come to Your peo - ple as we draw near. Hear us from heav -
C
C/B
Dm7
- en, touch our gen - er - a - tion. We are Your peo - ple, cry - ing out in
1
Fmaj7
2
Fmaj7
des - per - a - tion. des - per - a - tion.
O - pen the blind

GOD YOU REIGN

Words and Music by LINCOLN BREWSTER
and MIA FIELDES

You paint the night,
You part the seas,

You count the stars and You call them by name.
You move the mountains with the words that You say.

© 2008 INTEGRITY'S PRAISE MUSIC (BMI) and HILLSONG PUBLISHING (ASCAP)
INTEGRITY'S PRAISE MUSIC Admin.
HILLSONG PUBLISHING Admin. in the United States and Canada at EMICMGPUBLISHING.COM
All Rights Reserved   Used by Permission

Bm7
G
D
Dsus
The skies pro - claim: God, You reign.
My song re - mains: God, You reign.
D
Dsus
Your glo - ry shines,
You hold my life,
D
Dsus
Bm7
You teach the sun when to bring a new day. Cre - a - tion sings:
You know my heart and You call me by name. I live to say:
G
D
God, You reign.
God, You reign.
God, You

reign. God, You reign.

For-ev-er__ and ev-er, God, You

reign. reign.

God, You reign. God, You

Bm7
A
reign.
For - ev - er ___ and ev - er,
To Coda
G
D
God, You reign.
A/C♯
Em
D
Bm7
A/C♯
D
Hal - le - lu - jah, al - le - lu.
A/C♯
Em
D
Bm7
A
D
Hal - le - lu - jah, al - le - lu.

A/C♯
G/B
D/A
D/G
A
Hal - le - lu - jah, al - le -
D
A/C♯
G/B
D/A
lu. Hal - le - lu - jah,
D/E
A
D
D.S. al Coda
(take 2nd ending)
al - le - lu. God, You
CODA
D
G
reign. God, You reign.

Bm7
God, You reign.
For - ev - er and
A
G
ev - er,
God, You reign.
1
D
reign.
2
D
Dsus
God, You reign.
D
Dsus
D

A GREATER SONG

Words and Music by MATT REDMAN
and PAUL BALOCHE

With praise

Who could imagine a melody
Who could imagine a symphony
true enough to tell of Your mercy?
grand enough to tell of Your glory?
Who could imagine a harmony
Our highest praise but a feeble breath, a

© 2006 INTEGRITY'S HOSANNA! MUSIC (ASCAP) and THANKYOU MUSIC (PRS)
INTEGRITY'S HOSANNA! MUSIC Admin. at EMICMGPUBLISHING.COM
THANKYOU MUSIC Admin. Worldwide at EMICMGPUBLISHING.COM excluding Europe which is Admin. by Kingswaysongs
All Rights Reserved   Used by Permission

sweet e-nough to tell of Your love? ____
whis-per of Your thun-der-ous worth. ____ I see the heav-

-ens pro-claim-ing You day ____ af-ter day, and I know ____

____ in my heart ____ that there must ____ be a way ____ to sing a great-

-er song, _____ a great-er song to You on the earth. ____

Cmaj7
G
Bm/F♯
To sing a great - er song, a great -
Em
Cmaj7
D.S. al Coda
- er song to You on the earth.
CODA
G
Bm/F♯
to sing a great - er song, a great -
mf
Em
Cmaj7
G
- er song to You on the earth. To sing a great - er song,

Bm/F♯
Em
1
Cmaj7
a great - er song to You on the earth. To sing a great -
2
Cmaj7
G
D/F♯
Oh, hal - le - lu - jah! We wan-na lift You high - er.
f
Em7
1-3
C
4
C
Hal - le - lu - jah! We wan-na lift You high - er. We wan-na lift You high - er,
high - er, high - er.
dim.

I see the heavens proclaiming You day ____ after day, and I know ____

____ in my heart ____ that there must ____ be a way. ____

Hal - le - lu - jah! We wan - na lift You high - er.

1, 2
3
F
C
C
Hal - le - lu - jah! We wan - na lift You high - er. We wan - na lift You high - er.
A
E/G♯
F♯m7
Hal - le - lu - jah! We wan - na lift You high - er. Hal - le - lu - jah!
f
Repeat ad lib.
Final Ending
D
D
We wan - na lift You high - er. We wan - na lift You high - er.
rit.

HERE IN YOUR PRESENCE

Words and Music by
JON EGAN

Found in Your hands, fullness of joy, every fear suddenly wiped away, here in Your presence.

© 2006 VERTICAL WORSHIP SONGS (ASCAP)
Admin. at EMICMGPUBLISHING.COM
All Rights Reserved   Used by Permission

All of my gains now fade away, every crown no longer on display, here in Your presence. Heaven is trembling in awe of Your wonders, the kings and their kingdoms are standing amazed.

Here in Your presence, we are undone.

Guitar solo 3rd time (vocal tacet)

Here in Your presence, heaven and earth become one. Here in Your

D
A/C♯
pres - ence, all things are new.
Here in Your
Bm7
A
G
To Coda
1
D.C.
(no repeat)
pres - ence, ev - 'ry - thing bows be - fore You.
2
D.S.
3
N.C.

Won - der - ful, _____ beau - ti - ful, _____ glo - ri - ous, _____ match - less in ev - 'ry way. Won - der - ful, ____ beau - ti - ful, _____ glo - ri - ous, _____ match - less in ev - 'ry way.

Bm7
A
Gmaj7
Won - der - ful, ___ beau - ti - ful, ___ glo - ri - ous, ___
1
2
F♯m7
G6
D/A
F♯m7
G
match - less in ev - 'ry way. match - less in ev - 'ry way. ___
A
D.S. al Coda
CODA
D
___ Here in Your
Here in Your pres - ence.

HOLY GOD

Words and Music by
BRIAN DOERKSEN

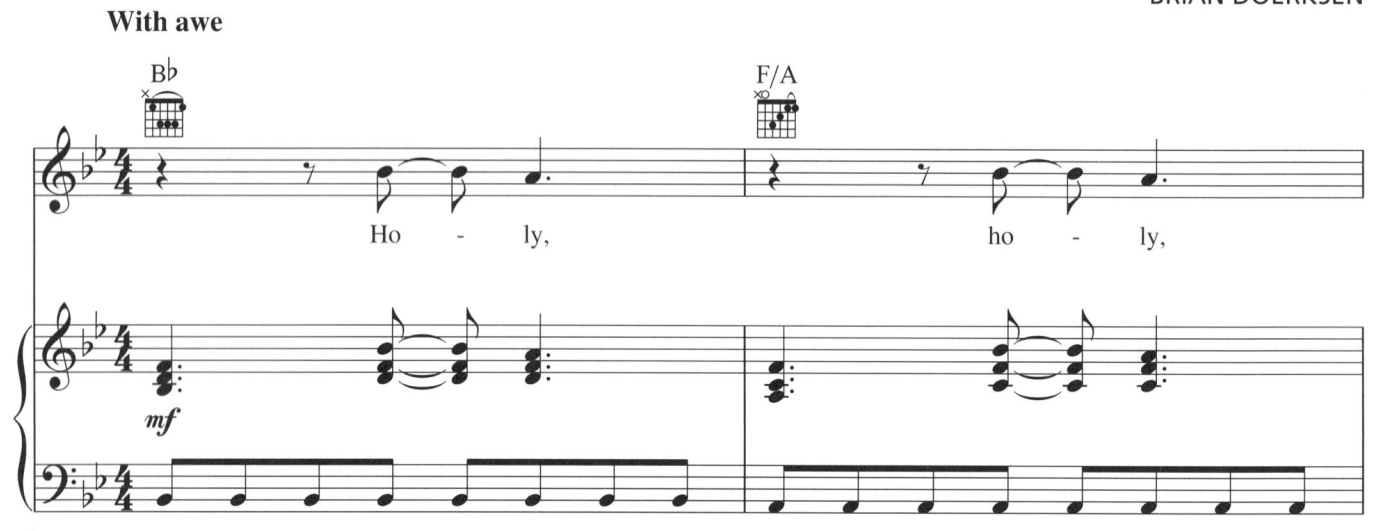

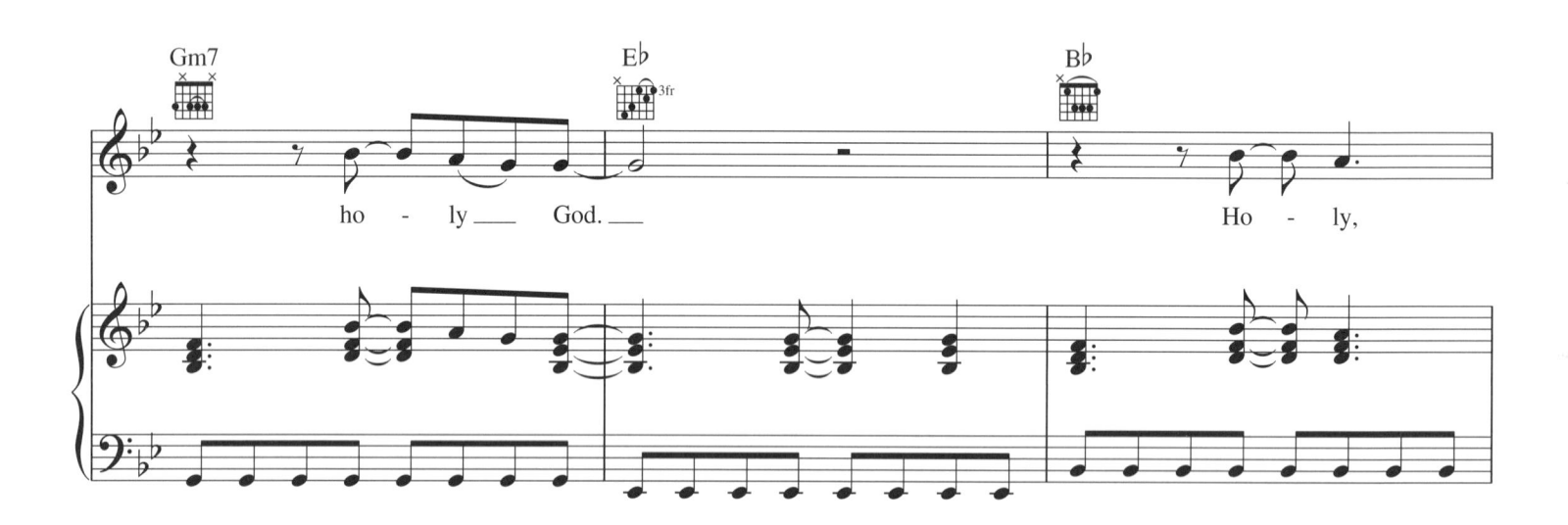

With awe

Ho - ly, ho - ly, ho - ly ___ God. ___ Ho - ly, ho - ly, ho - ly ___ God. ___

Cre - at -
For - giv -

-ing, com - mand - ing, tran - scen - dent A - do - nai.
-ing, re - deem - ing from ev - 'ry tribe and tongue.

De - fend - ing love, de - stroy - ing sin, the War-
A - ris - ing first, the nail - scarred Lamb, sal - va-

-ri - or di - vine.
-tion's Cham - pi - on.

D.C. al Coda

CODA

Ro - manc - ing, pur - su-

-ing, re-claim-ing to re-store. Re-leas-ing hearts, trans-form-ing lives, the Li-on's might-y roar. Ho-ly, ho-ly, ho-ly God. Ho-ly,

79

Ro - manc - ing, pur-su- ing, re - claim - ing to ____ re - store. ____ Re - leas - ing hearts, trans - form - ing lives, __ the Li - on's might - y roar. __

81

HOSANNA
(Praise Is Rising)

Words and Music by PAUL BALOCHE
and BRENTON BROWN

With a driving beat

C
N.C.
we turn to You.
we turn to You.
f
G
Hope is stir - ring,
In Your king - dom
mf
C
hearts are yearn - ing for You,
bro - ken lives are re - newed;
N.C.
we long for You.
You make us new.
'Cause when we see
f

You, we find strength to face the day.

In Your pres-ence, all our fears are washed a-way,

washed a-way. Ho-san-na, ho-san-na! You are the God

who saves us, worthy of all our praises. Ho-san-na, ho-san-na! Come, have Your way a-mong us. We wel-come You here,

Lord Je - sus.

Ho - san - na!

Ho-sanna! Ho-sanna, ho-sanna, ho-sanna, ho-sanna. Ho-sanna, ho-

C
san - na! Come, have Your way
Em
D
a - mong us. We wel - come You here,
Am7
C
E5
Lord Je - sus.
D
Am7
C6
Ho - san - na!

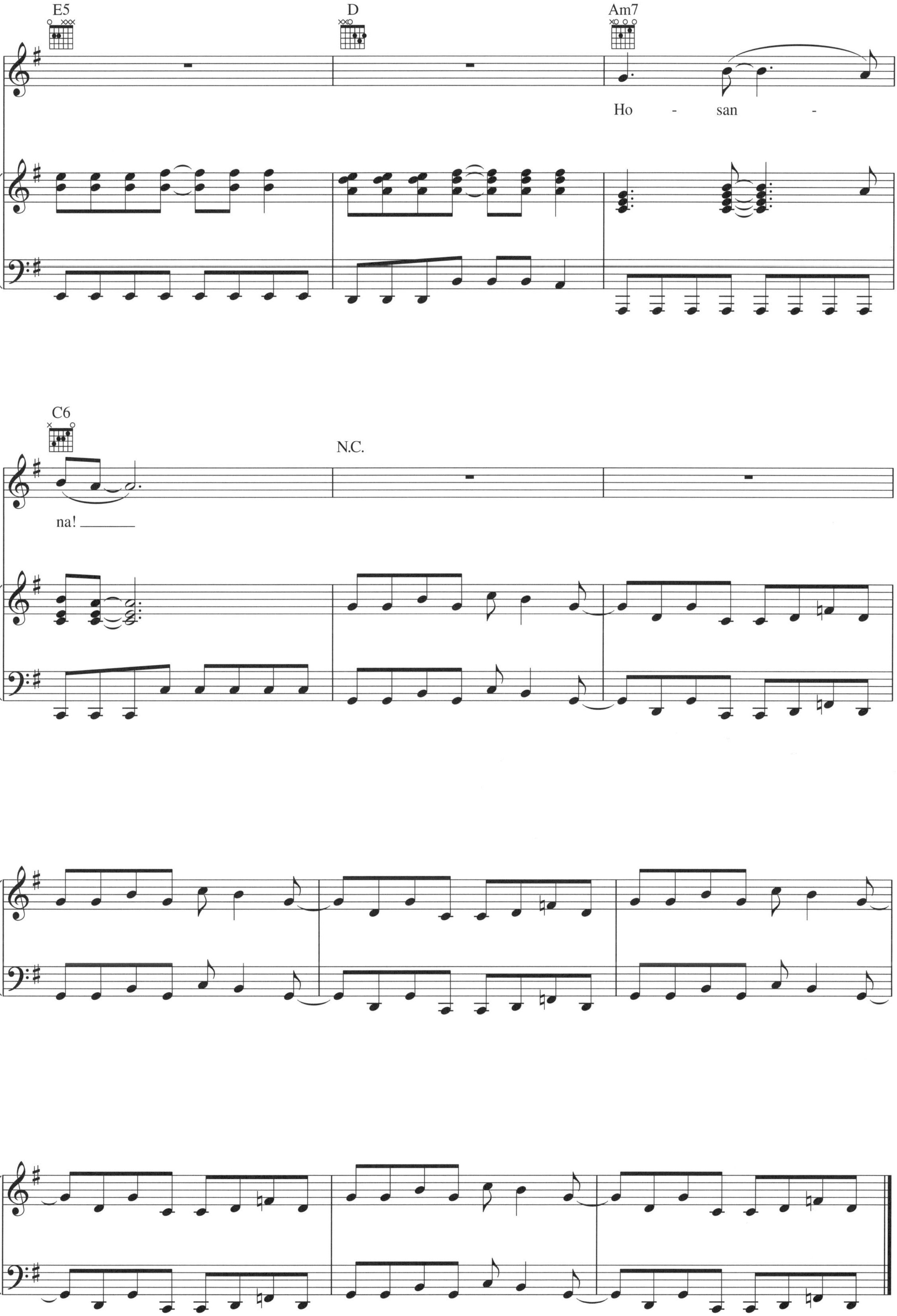
E5
D
Am7
Ho - san -
C6
N.C.
na!

HOW HE LOVES

Words and Music by
JOHN MARK McMILLAN

Slowly, in 2

He is jealous for me.

Loves like a hurricane; I am a tree, bending beneath the weight of His wind and mercy.

© 2005 INTEGRITY'S HOSANNA! MUSIC (ASCAP)
Admin. at EMICMGPUBLISHING.COM
All Rights Reserved   Used by Permission

And all of a sudden, I am unaware of these afflictions eclipsed by glory, and I realize just how beautiful You are, and how great Your affections are for me. And oh,

how He ___ loves us. ___ Oh, oh, how He ___ loves ___ us, ___ how He ___ loves us _____ all.

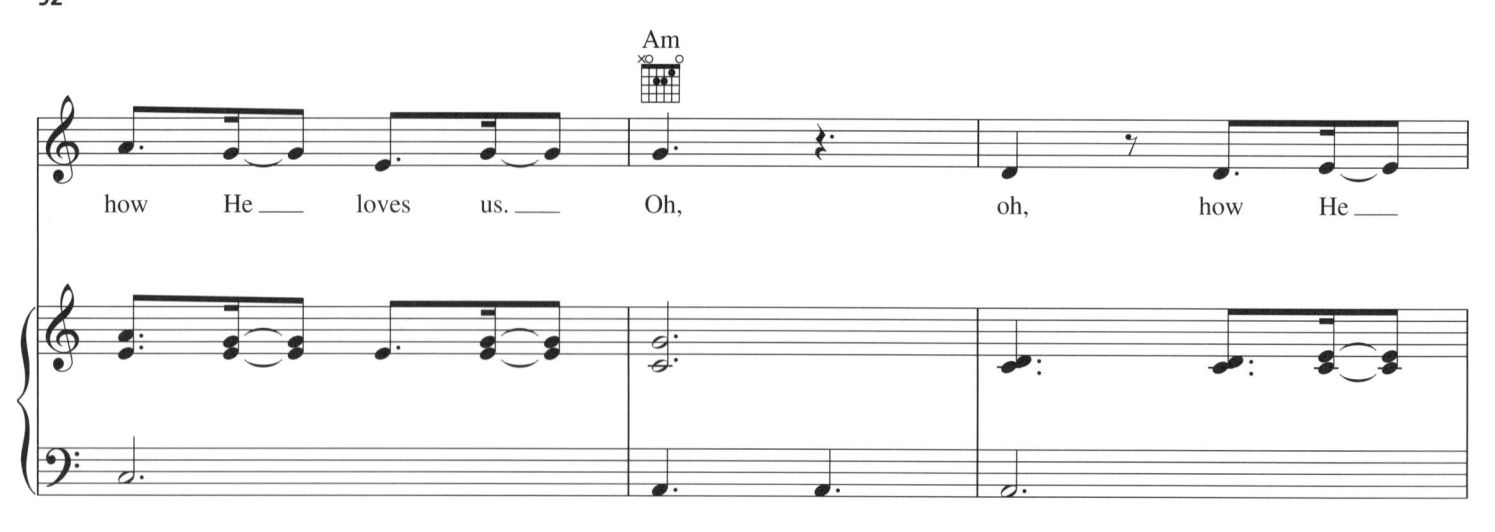

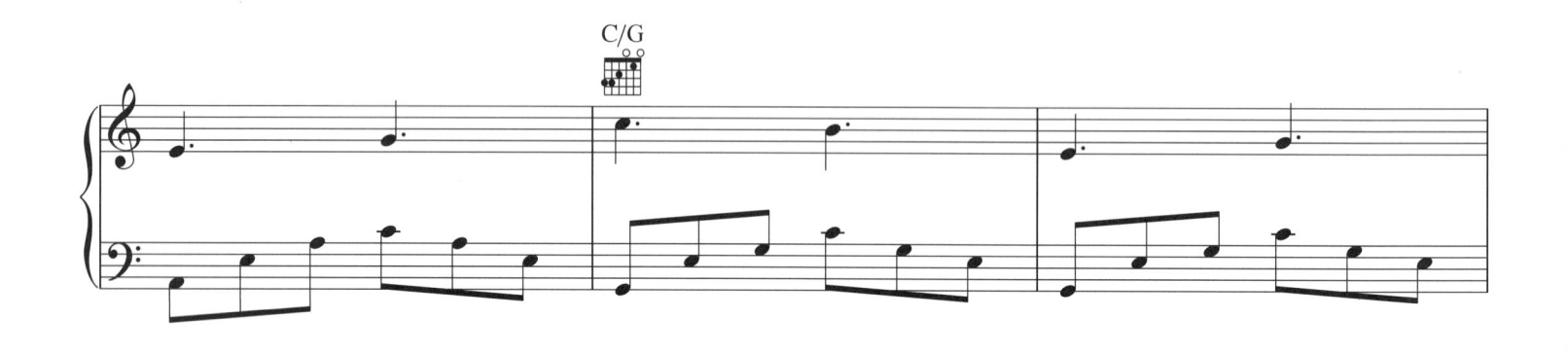

loves us. Oh, how He loves us. Oh, how He loves us. Oh, how He loves. And we are His portion and

Yeah, He

Am
He is our prize, drawn to redemption by the grace in His eyes. If His

C/G **F**
grace is an ocean, we're all sinking.

C
And heaven meets earth like an unforeseen kiss, and my

Am **C/G**
heart turns violently inside of my chest. I don't have time to main-

tain these re-grets__ when I think a-bout the way__ that He

loves us. Oh,_____ how He loves us.

Oh,_____ how He loves us. Oh,_____ how He

loves._____ Yeah, He

[C] [Am]

[C/G] [F(add9)]

Yeah, He

[C] loves us. Oh, _____ how He loves us. [Am] Oh, _____ how He

[C/G] loves us. Oh, _____ how He [F5] loves.

I WILL BOAST

Words and Music by
PAUL BALOCHE

Let not the wise___ man boast in his wis- -dom or the strong___ man boast in his strength. Let not the rich___

© 2006 INTEGRITY'S HOSANNA! MUSIC (ASCAP)
Admin. at EMICMGPUBLISHING.COM
All Rights Reserved   Used by Permission

___ man boast in his rich-es, but let the hum-ble come and give thanks to the One who ___ made ___ us, the One who ___ saved ___ us. I will boast in the Lord my God, I will boast in the One who's wor-thy.

D
A
Asus
Bm
I will boast in the Lord my God, I will boast in the
A
E7
G
One who's wor - thy. He is wor - thy.
D
A5
5fr
D
Let not the wise man boast in his wis - dom or the strong
mf

man boast in his strength. Let not the rich man boast in his riches, but let the humble come and give thanks to the One who made us, the One who saved us. I will boast in the Lord my God,

| Bm | A | D |

I will boast in the One who's wor-thy. I will boast in the

| A Asus | Bm | 1. A |

Lord my God, I will boast in the One who's wor-thy.

| 2. A | E7 | G |

One who's wor-thy. He's wor-thy.

| Bm | D | E7 |

I will make my boast in Christ a-lone.

D
F♯m/C♯
Bm
I will make my boast in Christ a - lone.
mf
1
G
2
G
D
I will make my boast
f
F♯m/E
Bm
G
in Christ a - lone.
D
F♯m/C♯
Bm
I will make my boast in Christ a - lone.

G
D
I will boast in the Lord my God,
Bm
A
D
I will boast in the One who's wor - thy. I will boast in the
A
Asus
Bm
A
Lord my God, I will boast in the One who's wor - thy.

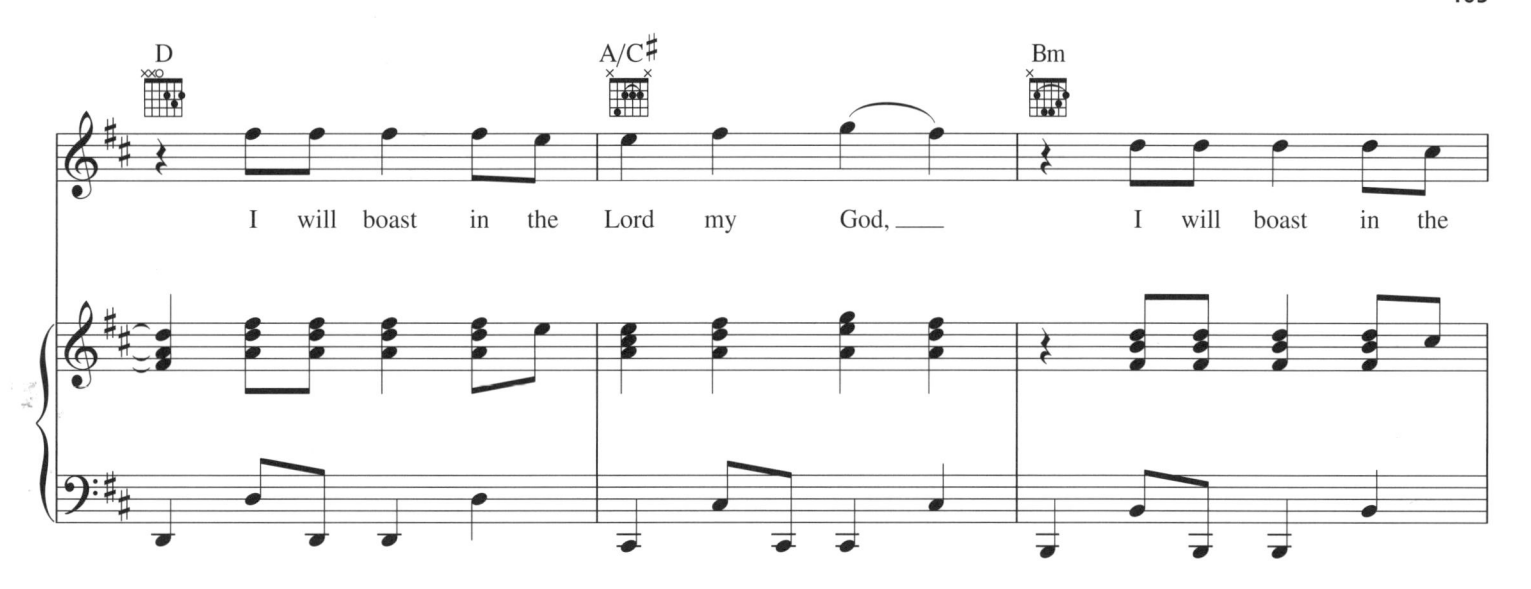

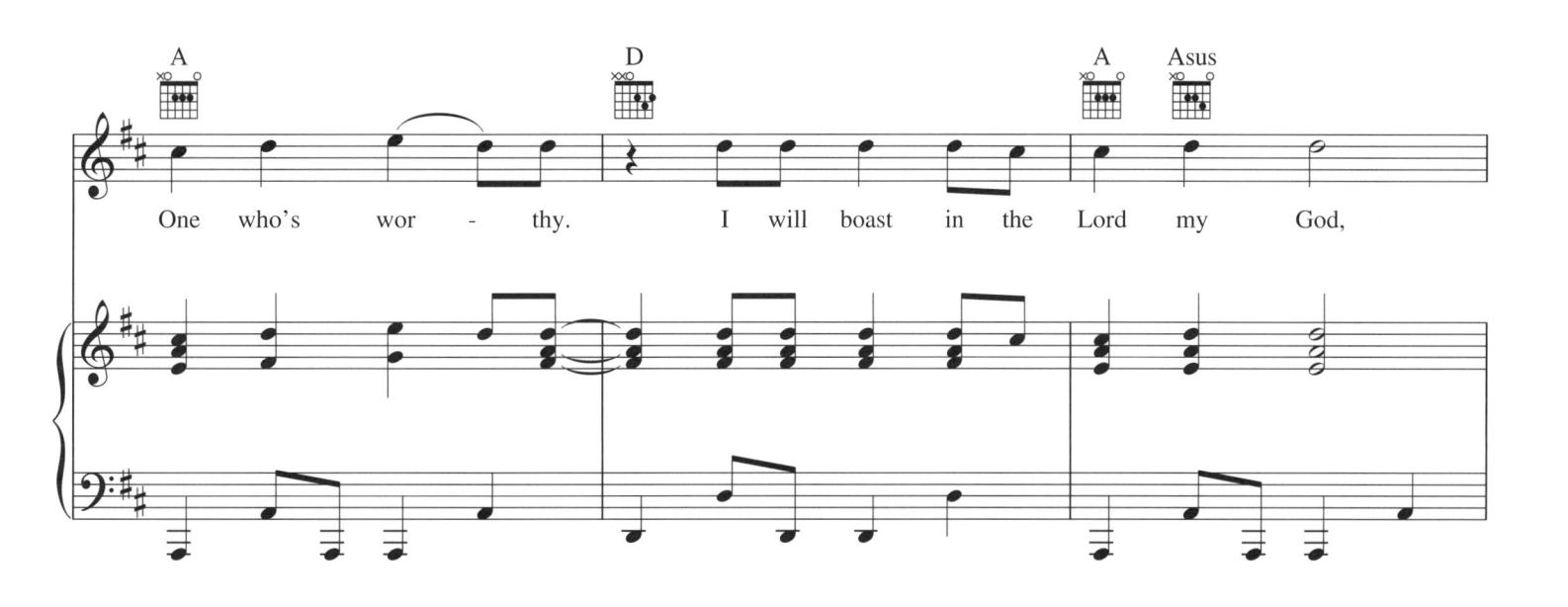

I will boast in the Lord my God, I will boast in the One who's wor-thy. I will boast in the Lord my God, I will boast in the One who's wor-thy.

I AM FREE

Words and Music by
JON EGAN

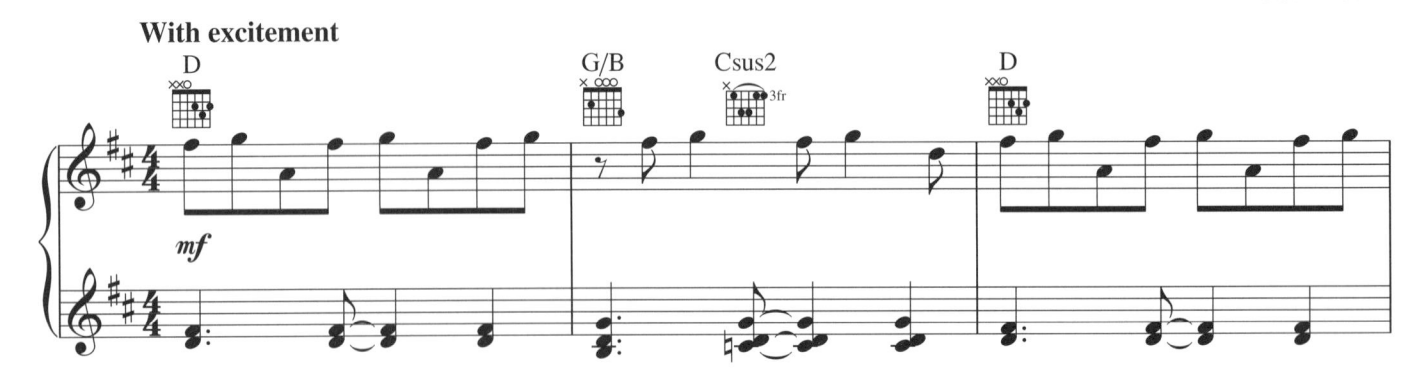

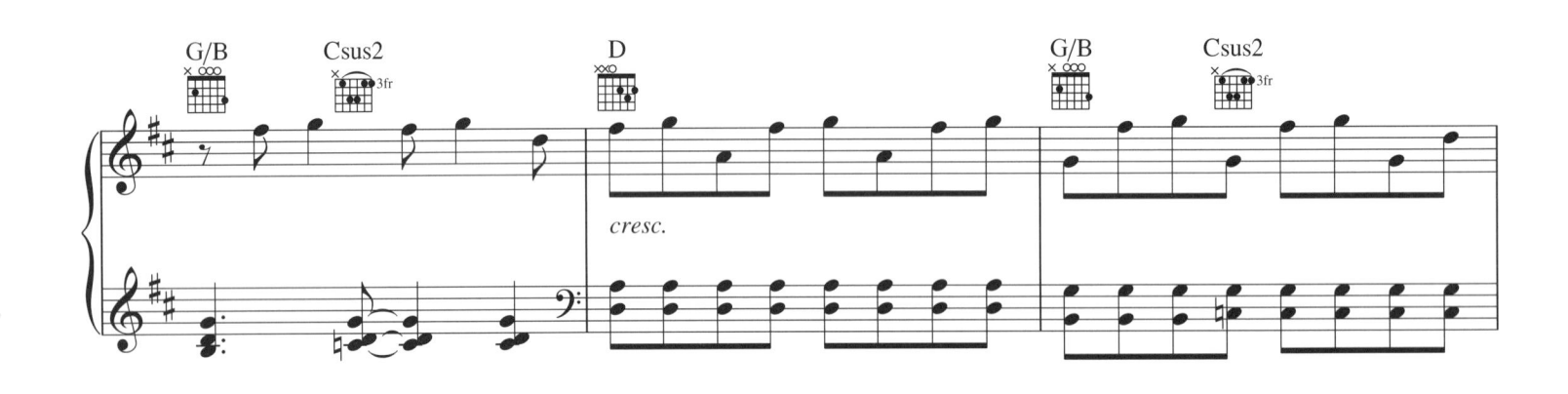

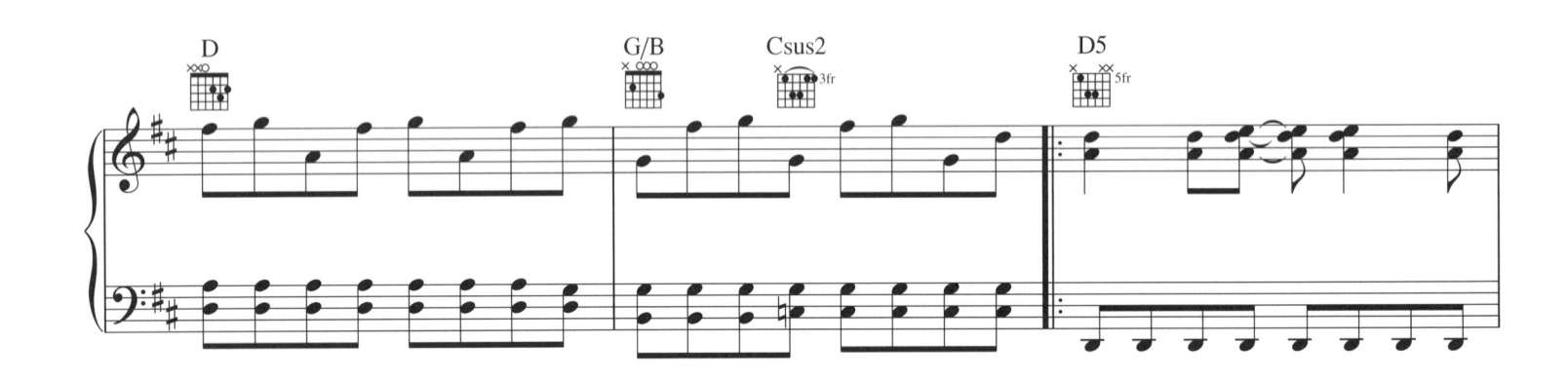

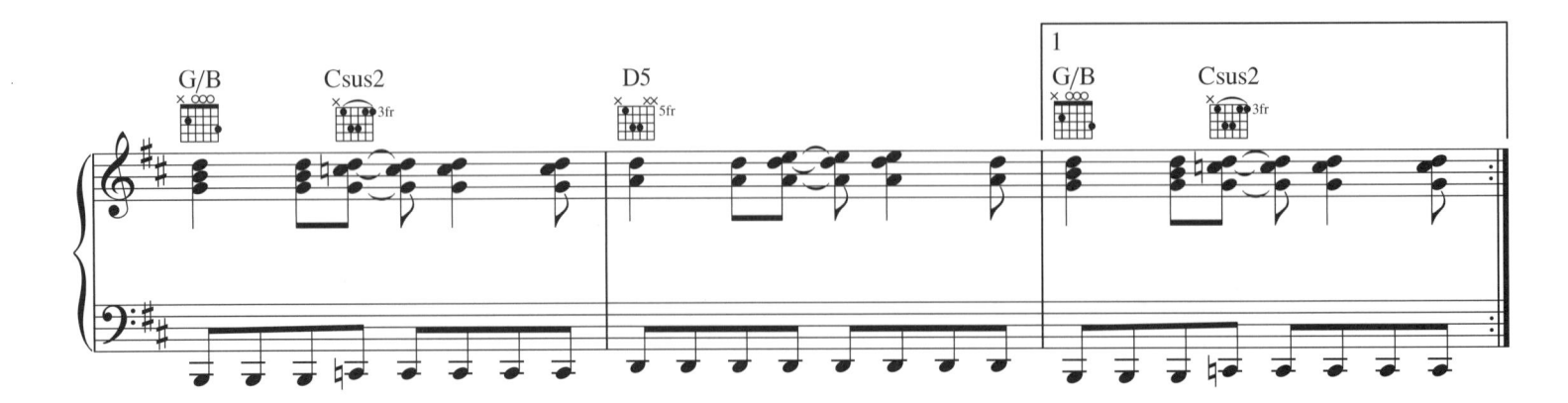

© 2004 VERTICAL WORSHIP SONGS (ASCAP)
Admin. at EMICMGPUBLISHING.COM
All Rights Reserved   Used by Permission

Through You the blind will see,
Lead vocal ad lib. on repeat
through You the mute will sing, through You the dead will rise, through You our hearts will praise, through You the darkness flees,

through You my heart screams, "I am free! I am free!" I am free to run. (I am free to run.) I am free to dance. (I am

Bm7
free to dance.) I am free to live for You.
Asus
To Coda
(I am free to live for You.) I am free.
Csus2
Em9
(I am free.) I am free. (I am free.)
1
D
G/B
Csus2

D
G/B
Csus2
3fr
2
D.S. al Coda
I am
CODA
D
I am free,
(I am free.)
I am free.
(I am free.)
mf

111

Gsus2
oh,
oh,
Bm7
Asus
oh.
I am free,
Csus2
Em7(add4)
yeah!
cresc.
D
Say-ing I am free.
(I am free to run.)
f

113

I NEED YOU MORE

Words and Music by
LINDELL COOLEY
and BRUCE HAYNES

I need ___ You ___ more, ___

© 1996 INTEGRITY'S HOSANNA! MUSIC (ASCAP) and CENTERGY MUSIC (BMI)
INTEGRITY'S HOSANNA! MUSIC Admin. at EMICMGPUBLISHING.COM
CENTERGY MUSIC Admin. by WORDS & MUSIC, COPYRIGHT ADMINISTRATION
All Rights Reserved   Used by Permission

more than yes-ter-day. I need You more, more than words can say. I need You more than ev-er be-fore. I need You, Lord,

Lyrics:

I need You, Lord. I need You more,

More than the air I breathe, more than the song I sing, more than the next heartbeat, more than anything. And, Lord, as time _goes by, ___ I'll ___ be by ___ Your side, ___ 'cause I nev-er want ___ to go ___ back ___ to my old life. ___ I need ___ You more, ___

D.S. al Coda

CODA

I need ___ You, Lord, ___ I need ___ You, ___ Lord.

JUST TO BE WITH YOU

Words and Music by JASON INGRAM
and PAUL BALOCHE

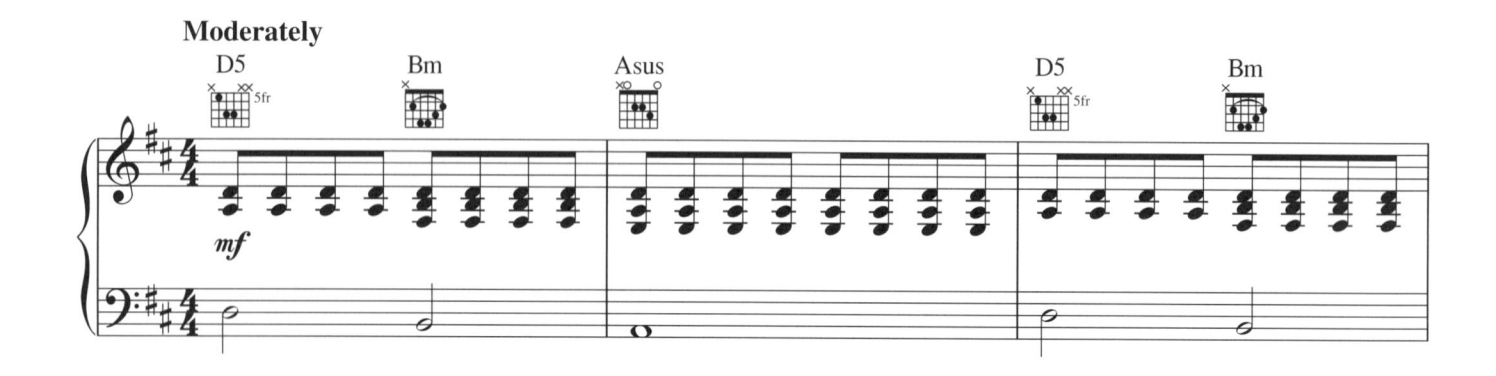

Lord, my life is an emp-ty cup. Here's my heart; would You fill me up? I'm face to the ground,

119

with You, just to be with You. I have come to the end of me, and there's nothing I have to bring. But You said I belong, You say I am Yours. Nothing compares to knowing You more. All I want,

CODA
G D
Oh, You made a way for me.
Bm A G Bm Asus
Oh, Sav - ior, I'm Yours for - ev - er - more. Oh,
G D Bm A
You made a way for me. Oh, Sav - ior,
G Bm Asus G Bm
I'm Yours for - ev - er - more. I'm Yours for - ev - er - more.

Asus A D
All I want, all I need
mp
Asus Bm7
is just to be with You, just to be
Gsus2 D A
with You. Here I am at Your feet, just to be
Bm7 Gsus2
with You, just to be with You. All I want,

D
Asus
Bm7
all I need is just to be with You, just to be
mf
Gsus2
D
A
with You. Here I am at Your feet, just to be
Bm7
1
Gsus2
2
Gsus2
with You, just to be with You. All I want, with You.
Oh, all I want is just to be with You.

LET THE PRAISES RING

Words and Music by
LINCOLN BREWSTER

With energy

O Lord my God, in You I put my trust.
my God, to You I give my hands.

© 2002 INTEGRITY'S PRAISE! MUSIC (BMI)
Admin. at EMICMGPUBLISHING.COM
All Rights Reserved Used by Permission

125

In You, in You I find my peace.

In You, in You I find my strength.

In You I live and move and breathe.

127

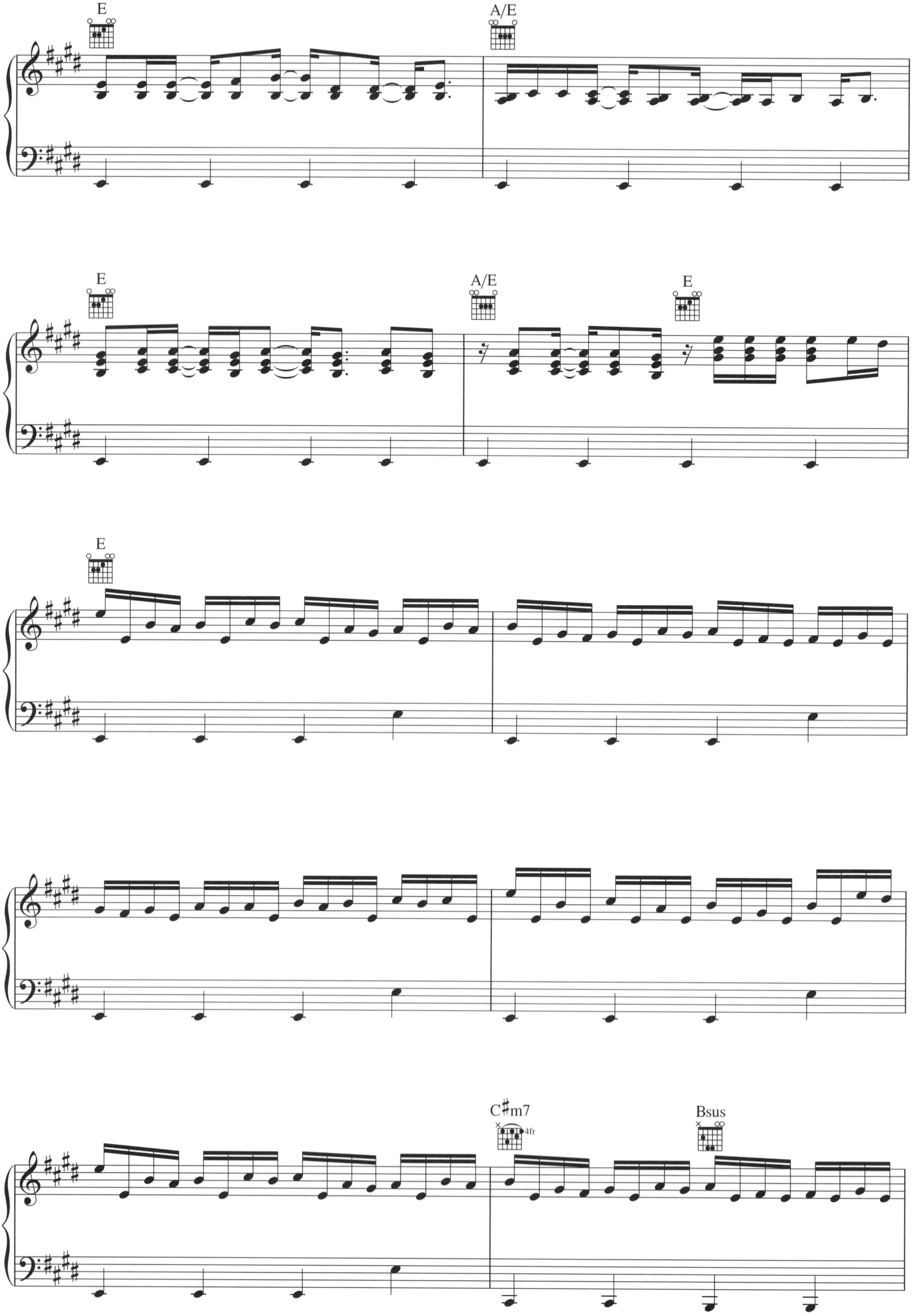
E
A/E
E
A/E
E
E
C♯m7
4fr
Bsus

129

I live and move and breathe. Let ev-'ry-thing I say and do be found-ed by my faith in You. I lift up ho-ly hands and sing. Let the prais-es ring!

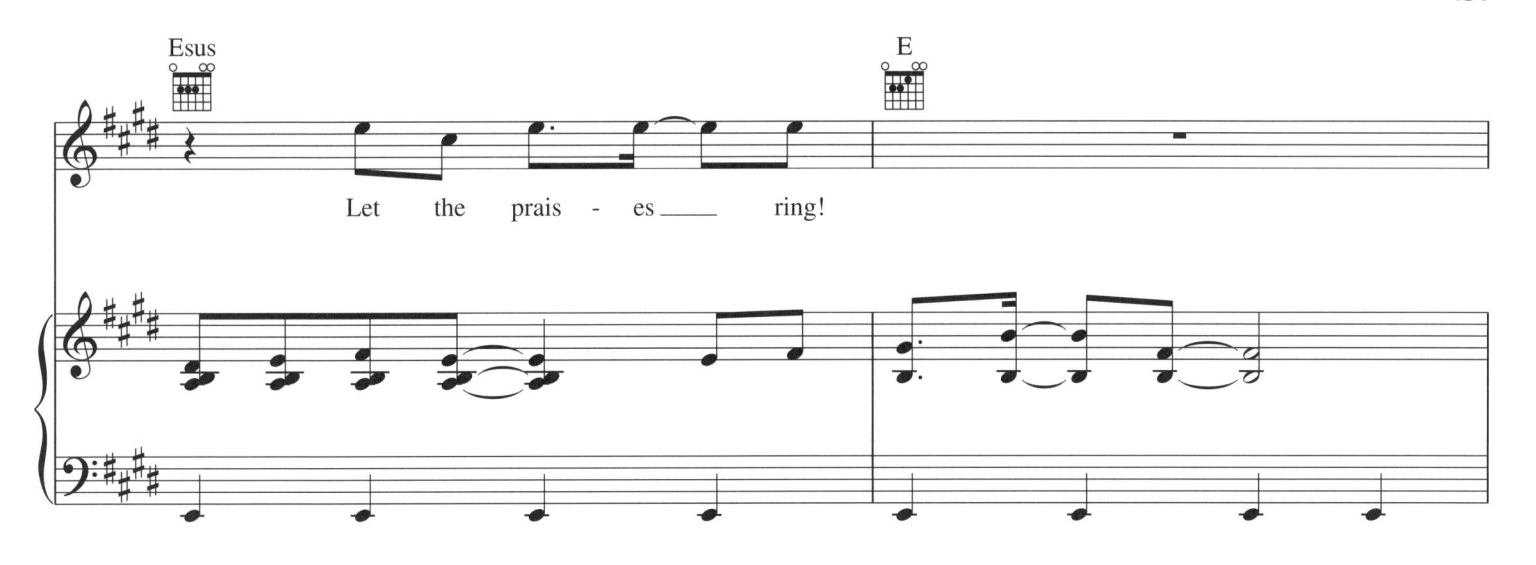

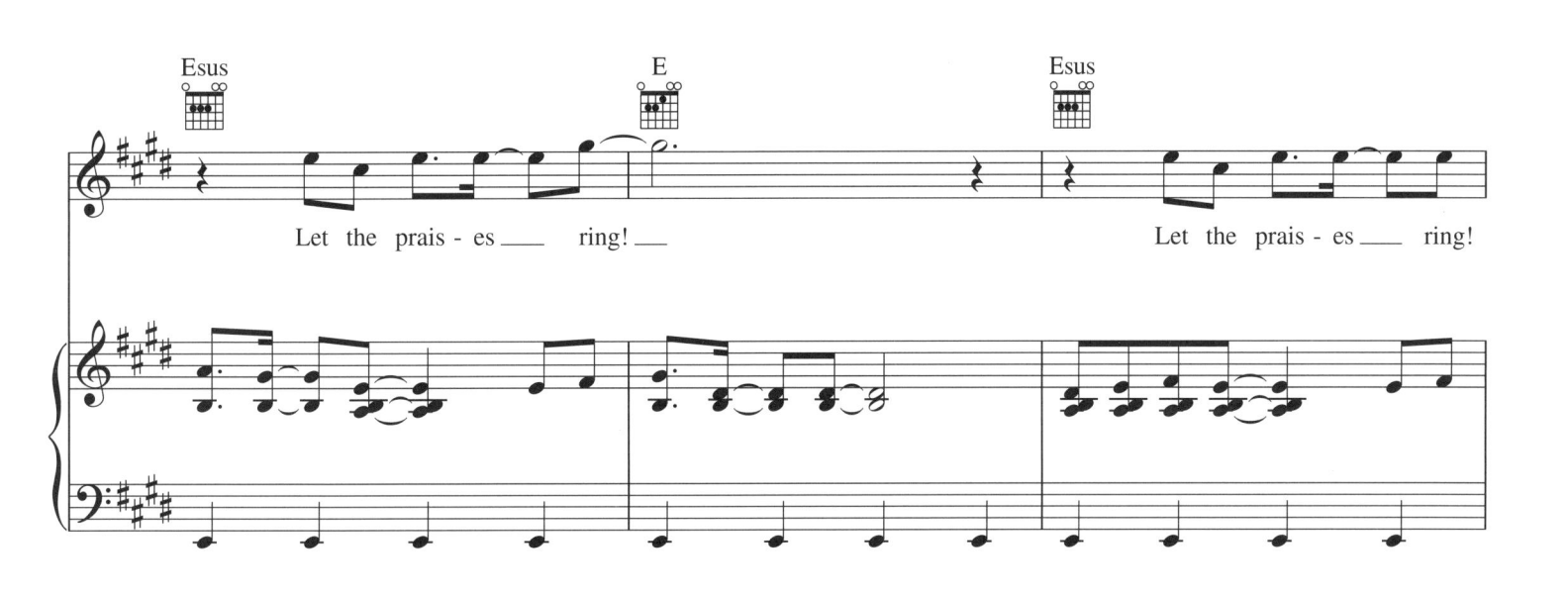

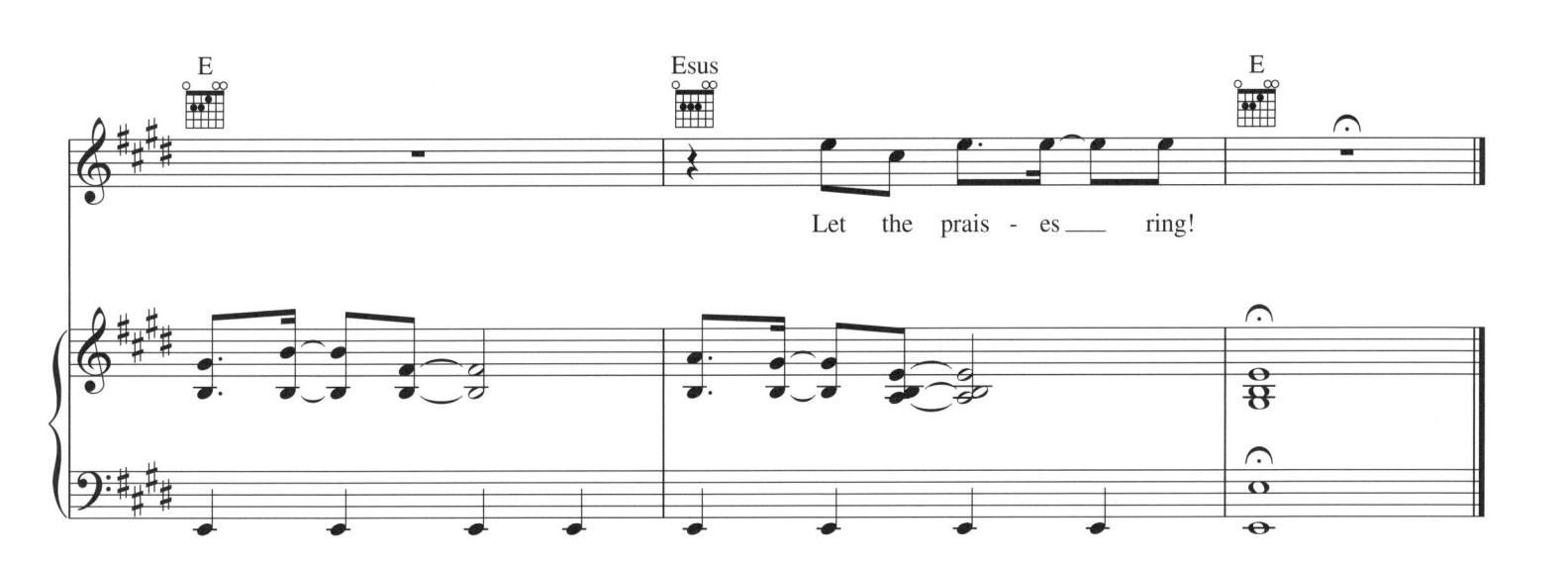

Let the prais - es ___ ring!

Let the prais - es ___ ring! ___ Let the prais - es ___ ring!

Let the prais - es ___ ring!

LORD HAVE MERCY

Words and Music by
STEVE MERKEL

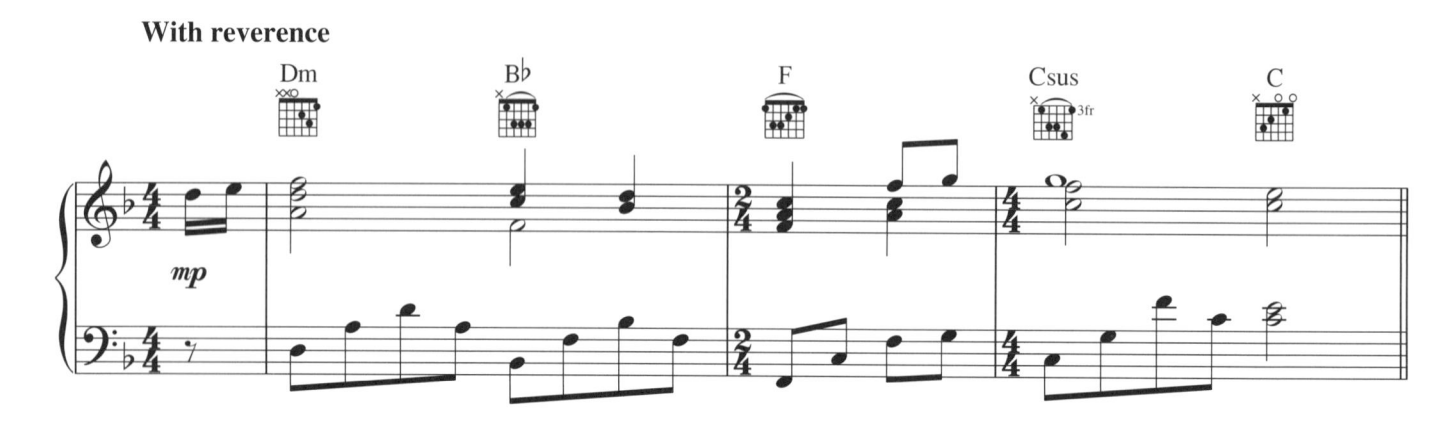

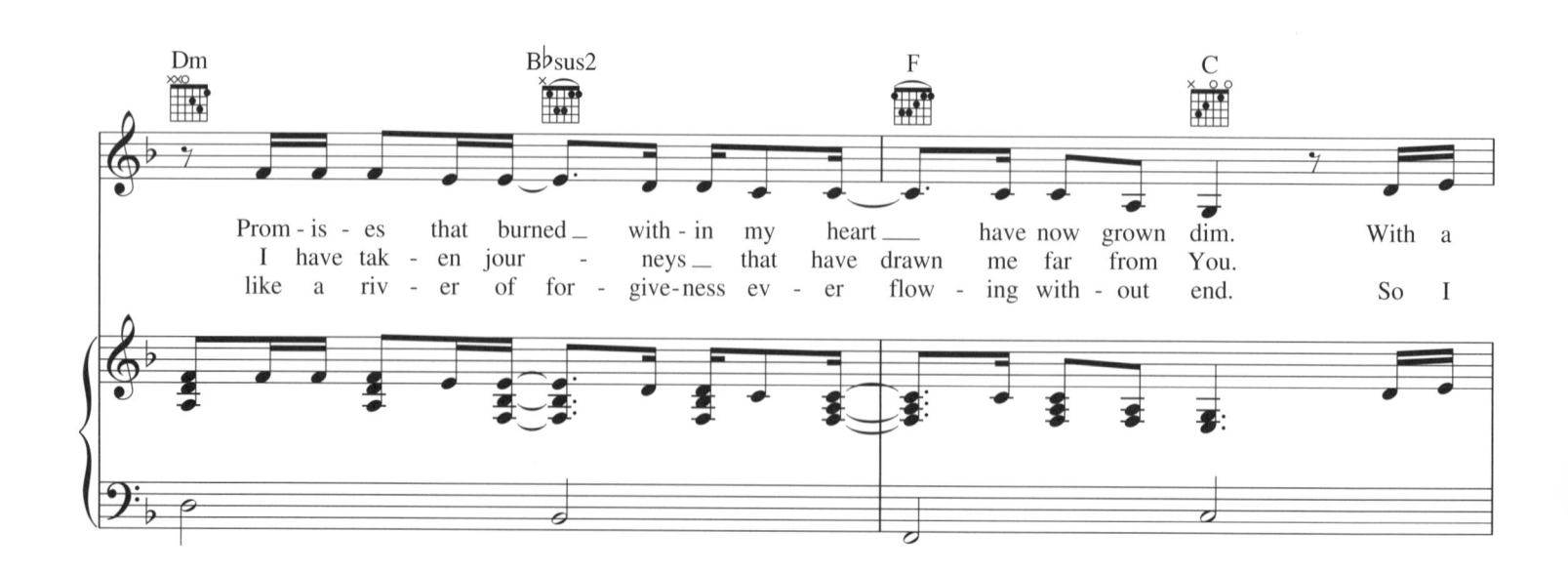

With reverence

Jesus, I've for-got-ten the words that You have spo-ken.
I have built an al-tar where I wor-ship things of man,
I have longed to know You and all Your ten-der mer-cies,

Prom-is-es that burned with-in my heart have now grown dim. With a
I have tak-en jour-neys that have drawn me far from You.
like a riv-er of for-give-ness ev-er flow-ing with-out end. So I

© 2000 INTEGRITY'S HOSANNA! MUSIC (ASCAP)
Admin. at EMICMGPUBLISHING.COM
All Rights Reserved Used by Permission

doubt-ing heart_ I fol-low the paths of earth-ly wis-dom._
So now I am re-turn-ing to Your mer-cies ev - er flow-ing._
bow my heart_ be-fore_ You in the good-ness of_ Your pres-ence,_

For-give me for my un-be-lief,_ re-new the fire_ a-
Par-don my trans-gres-sions,_ help me love You_ a-
Your grace for-ev-er shin-ing_ like a bea-con in_ the

gain.
gain.
night.   Lord have mer - cy, Christ have mer - cy,

Lord have mer - cy on_ me.   Lord have mer - cy,

Christ have mer - cy, Lord have mer - cy on ____ me.

me.

D.S. al Coda

CODA
B♭maj7 C F Gm C7/E Fsus F
on me. Lord have mer - cy,
F/A B♭maj7 C/E Dm Gm C7/E Fsus F
Christ have mer - cy, Lord have mer - cy
B♭maj7 Csus C Gm C7/E Fsus F F/A B♭maj7 C/E Dm
on me. Lord have mer - cy, Christ have mer - cy,
Gm C7/E Fsus F B♭maj7 C Fsus F
Lord have mer - cy on me.
rit.

LOVE THE LORD

Words and Music by
LINCOLN BREWSTER

Joyfully

Da da dum da da dum da da da. Da da dum da da dum da da da.

Da da dum oh, yeah.

Love the Lord your God with all your heart, with all your soul, with all your mind
I will serve the Lord with all my heart, with all my soul, with all my mind

© 2005 INTEGRITY'S PRAISE! MUSIC (BMI)
Admin. at EMICMGPUBLISHING.COM
All Rights Reserved Used by Permission

Csus2 3fr D G D Csus2 3fr
and with all your strength.
and with all my strength.
G D Em7 G/B
Love the Lord your God with all your heart, with all your soul, with all your mind
I will serve the Lord with all my heart, with all my soul, with all my mind
Csus2 3fr D G N.C.
and with all your strength. With all your heart,
and with all my strength. With all my heart,
Csus2 3fr D
with all your soul, with all your mind,
with all my soul, with all my mind,

with all your strength.
with all my strength.

Love the Lord your God with all your heart, with all your soul, with all your mind
I will serve the Lord with all my heart, with all my soul, with all my mind

and with all your strength. I will love You, Lord.
and with all my strength.

Da da dum da da dum da da da. Da da dum da da dum da da da.

Da da dum oh, yeah.

I will serve You.

La da da. Doo doo doo da da dee da da da da da da da.

With all my heart, with all my soul, with all my mind, with all my strength. With all my heart, with all my soul,

D
Csus2/E
with all my mind, oh, with all my strength.
D/F#
G
D
I will love You, Lord, with all my heart,
Em7
G/B
Csus2
D
with all my soul, with all my mind and with all my strength.
G
D
Csus2
G
D
I will love You, Lord, with all my heart,

with all my soul, with all my mind and with all my strength.

I will love You. Da da dum da da dum da da da.
(Lead vocal ad lib.)

Da da dum da da dum da da da. Da da dum oh, yeah.

Da da dum da da dum da da da.

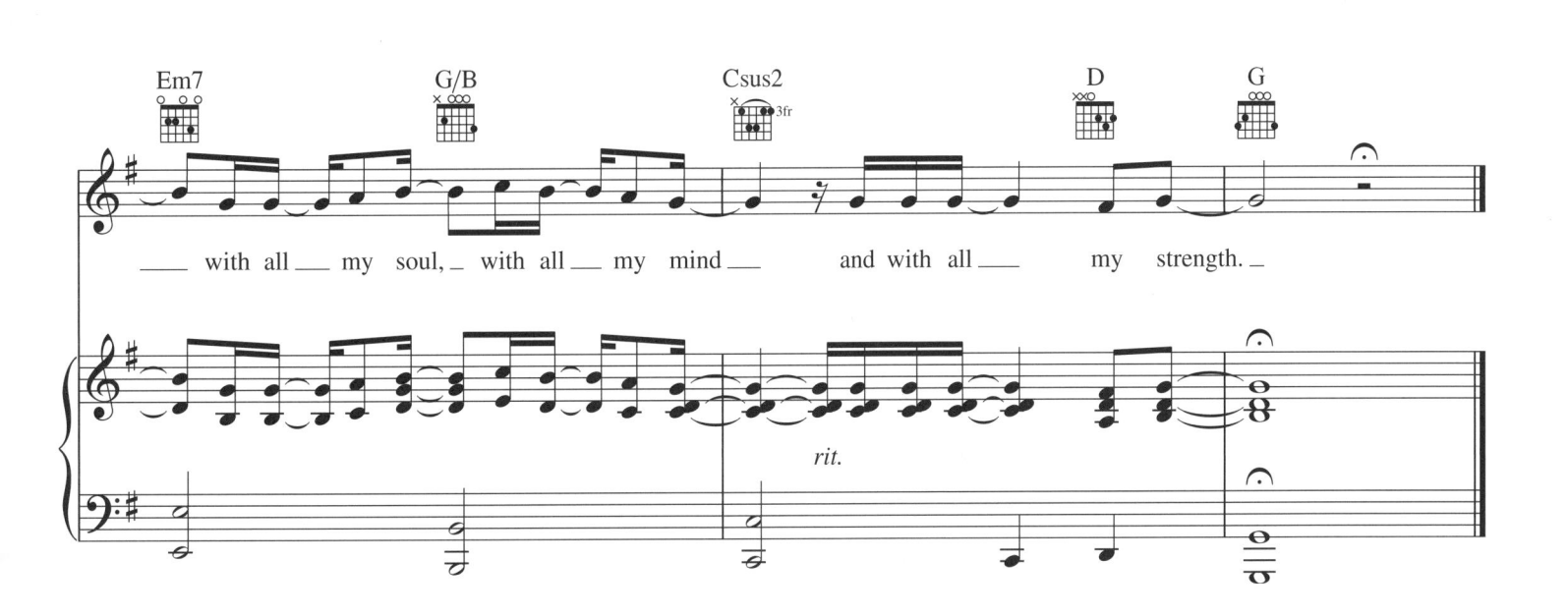

Da da dum da da dum da da da. Da da dum oh, yeah.

I will love You, Lord, with all my heart,

with all my soul, with all my mind and with all my strength.

rit.

MERCY

Words and Music by MARK HALL,
OMEGA LEVINE, SAM DE LONG
and TAUESE TOFA

Moderately

Here I am, a sinner, broken and in need of You.

Take my life and wash my fears away.

© 2009 INTEGRITY'S PRAISE! MUSIC (BMI), SONY/ATV MUSIC PUBLISHING LLC (BMI), CLUB ZOO MUSIC (BMI), MY REFUGE MUSIC (BMI) and PARACHUTE MUSIC (APRA)
INTEGRITY'S PRAISE! MUSIC, SONY/ATV MUSIC PUBLISHING LLC, CLUB ZOO MUSIC and MY REFUGE MUSIC Admin. at EMICMGPUBLISHING.COM
PARACHUTE MUSIC Admin. in the United States and Canada at EMICMGPUBLISHING.COM
All Rights Reserved   Used by Permission

Cm
A♭/C
Fm
3fr
For You are the great I AM. Rest as-sured, I feel Your hand
Cm
A♭/C
Fm
holding me until the dark-ness clears. A Fa-ther to the fa-
A♭
B♭
4fr
-ther-less, Re-deem-er of my soul. My life is Yours for-ev-
Cm
B♭/D
-er. My heart will al-ways know Your
mf

E♭
B♭/D
A♭
A♭maj7
mer - cy saved me. Mer - cy made me whole.
A♭
A♭maj7
E♭
B♭/D
Your mer - cy found me, called me as Your own.
A♭
A♭maj7
A♭
A♭maj7
Cm
Here I stand, a child of Yours,
A♭/C
Fm/C
Cm
bro - ken and in need of You. Break these chains and wash my guilt a - way.

Heal-er of my bro-ken-ness, my wea-ry soul will find its rest. You are my strength, the lift-er of my head. You're great-er than my yes-ter-days. You hold me close to-day. You're the Lord of my to-mor-rows. My heart will al-ways say:

You're greater than my yesterdays. You hold me close today. You're the Lord of my tomorrows. My heart will always say:

Your mercy saved me. Mercy made me whole.

Your mercy found me,

B♭/D
A♭
1
called me as Your own.
Your
2
E♭/G
E♭/A♭
mp
Cm
B♭7
You called me as Your own.
E♭/G
A♭
You called me as Your own.
You called me as Your own.

You called me as Your own.

cresc. poco a poco

You called me as Your own. Called me as Your own.

Thank You for Your mer - cy.

Thank You for Your mer - cy. Your

mer-cy _____ saved _____ me. Mer-cy made me whole. _____

Your mer-cy _____ found _____ me, called me as Your own. _____

Your You called me as _____ Your own, _____

Your own. _____

THE MORE I SEEK YOU

Words and Music by
ZACH NEESE

© 1999 GATEWAY CREATE PUBLISHING (BMI)
Admin. at EMICMGPUBLISHING.COM
All Rights Reserved   Used by Permission

153

Lyrics:
The more I find You, the more I love You. I want to sit at Your feet, drink from the cup in Your hand, lay back against You and breathe, feel Your heart-beat. This love is so deep, it's more than I can stand.

I melt in Your peace; it's o-ver-whelm-ing.

The more I seek You, the more I find You. The more I

155

find You, _____ the more _ I love You.

I want to sit at __ Your feet, drink from the cup in __ Your hand,

lay back a-gainst You __ and breathe, ___ feel Your heart-beat. __

This love is __ so deep, ___ it's more than I __ can stand. _

C♯m
1
A(add2)
Bsus
B
4fr
I melt in Your peace; it's o - ver - whelm - ing.
2
A(add2)
Bsus
C♯m7
B/D♯
E
A(add2)
it's o - ver - whelm - ing.
Oh, Your
mf
C♯m7
B/D♯
E
A
love is o - ver - whelm - ing me.
And,
C♯m7
B/D♯
E
A
Bsus
B
oh, my Lord, Your love is o - ver - whelm - ing me, o - ver -

A(add2)
E
whelm - ing me.
I want to sit at Your feet,
mp
B/D♯
4fr
C♯m
4fr
A(add2)
Bsus
B
drink from the cup in Your hand,
lay back a-gainst You and breathe,
feel Your heart - beat.
E
B/D♯
4fr
This love is so deep,
it's more than I can stand.
C♯m
4fr
A(add2)
Bsus
B
E(add2)
I melt in Your peace.
rit.

MOVING FORWARD

Words and Music by ISRAEL HOUGHTON
and RICARDO SANCHEZ

With movement

Not going back, I'm moving ahead. I'm here to declare to You my past is over. In You

© 2007 INTEGRITY'S HOSANNA! MUSIC (ASCAP), NEW BREED EXTENDED (ASCAP), RICARDO MUSIC DOT COM (ASCAP),
INTEGRITY'S PRAISE! MUSIC (BMI) and SOUND OF THE NEW BREED (BMI)
Admin. at EMICMGPUBLISHING.COM
All Rights Reserved   Used by Permission

A
Em7
F♯m7
all things are made new.
Surrendered my life to Christ, I'm
G
D
E/D
Dmaj7
E/D
D
E/D
moving, moving forward.
Oh.
F♯m
E/F♯
E
A
G
A
F♯m7
What a moment You have brought me to. Such a freedom

I have found in You. You're the healer who makes all things new, yeah, yeah, yeah.

Not going back, I'm moving ahead. I'm here to declare to You my past is o-ver. In You all things are made new. Sur-ren-dered my life to Christ, I'm mov-ing, mov-ing for-ward. You have ris-en

with all pow-er in Your hands. You have giv-en me a sec-ond chance. Hal-le-lu-jah, hal-le-lu-jah. Yeah, yeah, yeah. Yeah, yeah, yeah. Not go-ing back,

moving... Not going back, I'm moving ahead. I'm here to declare to You my past is over. In You all things are made new. Surrendered my life to Christ, I'm moving, moving forward, for-ward. For-ward, for-ward. For-ward, for-ward.

165

MY SAVIOR LIVES

Words and Music by JON EGAN
and GLENN PACKIAM

Driving Rock

Our God will reign ___ for-ev-er, ___ and all the world ___ will know His name. ___ Ev-'ry-one ___ to-geth-er,
The King has come ___ from Heav-en, ___ and dark-ness trem-bles at His name. ___ Vic-to-ry ___ for-ev-er

Recorded a half step lower.

© 2006 VERTICAL WORSHIP SONGS (ASCAP)
Admin. at EMICMGPUBLISHING.COM
All Rights Reserved Used by Permission

sing the song____ of the re - deemed.____
is the song____ of the re - deemed.____

cresc.

I know that my____ Re - deem - er lives,

f

and now I stand____ on what____ He did. My Sav - ior,

my Sav - ior lives.____

C
Am7
Ev - 'ry day a brand - new chance to say, "Je - sus, You are
F
the on - ly way." My Sav - ior, my Sav - ior lives.
To Coda
C
B♭sus2
C
1
B♭sus2
2
B♭sus2
C
My Sav - ior lives, yeah.

169

170

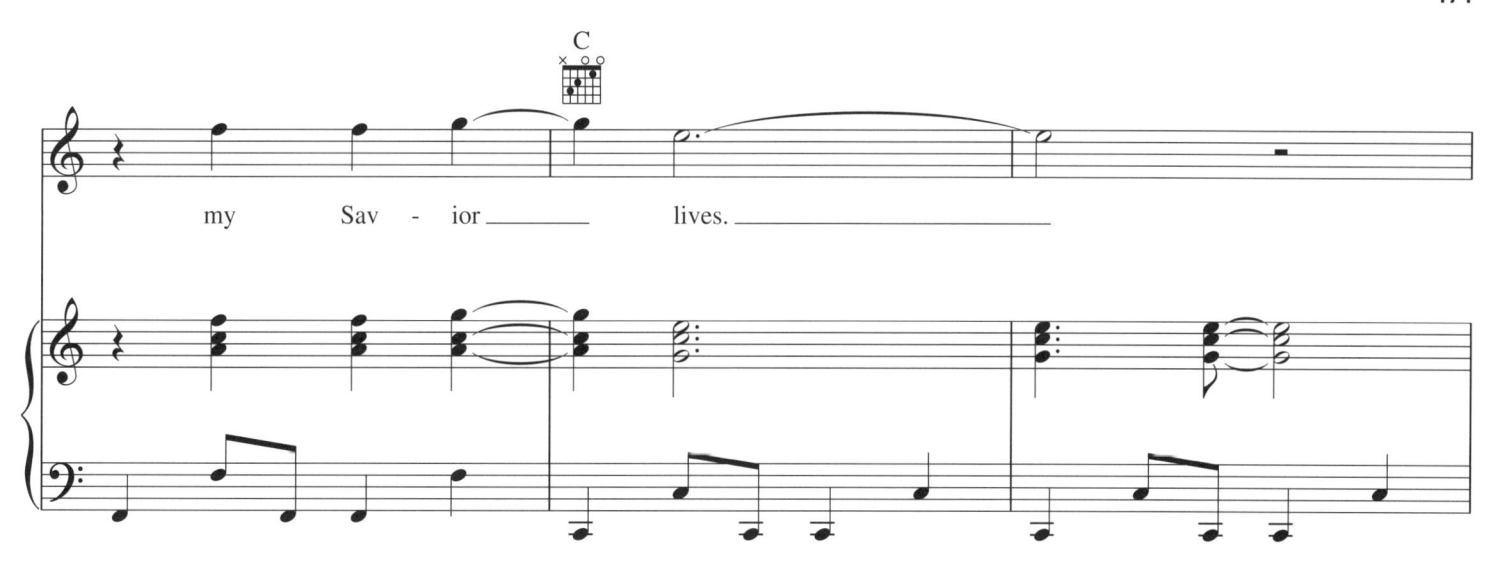

my Sav-ior lives.

My Sav-ior, my Sav-ior lives.

My Sav-ior, my Sav-ior lives.

NEW DOXOLOGY

Original Words and Music by *Genevan Psalter* and THOMAS KEN
New Lyrics and Chorus by THOMAS MILLER

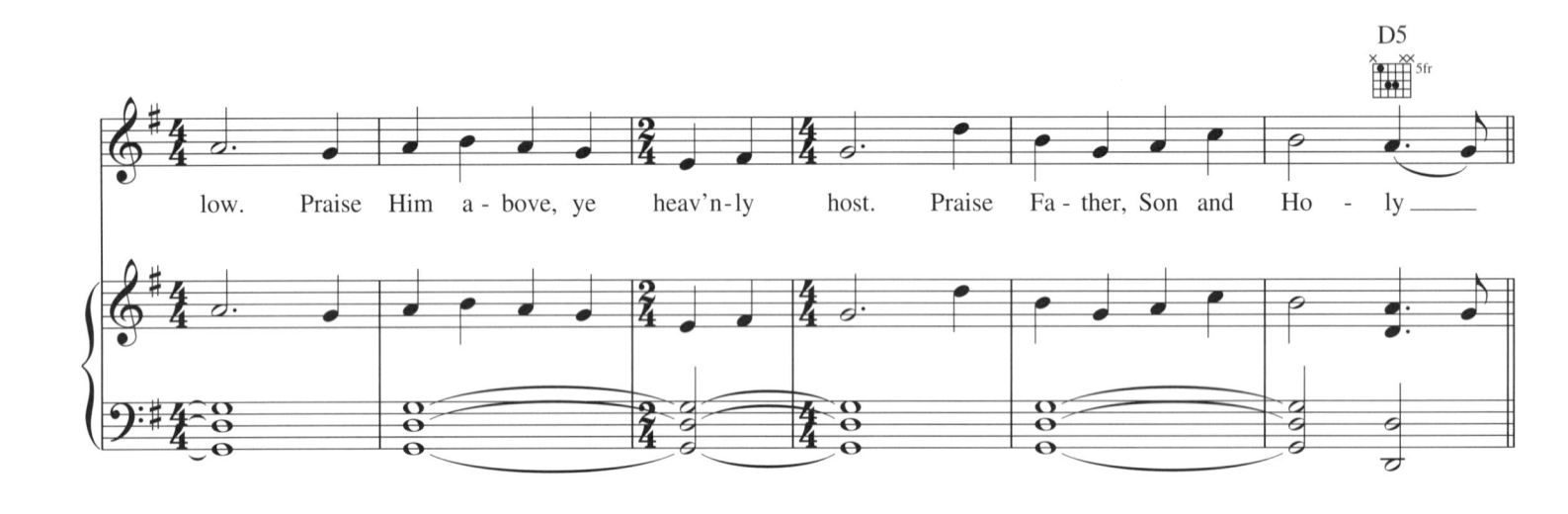

Reverently

Praise God, from whom all bless-ings flow. Praise Him, all crea-tures here be-low. Praise Him a-bove, ye heav'n-ly host. Praise Fa-ther, Son and Ho-ly Ghost.

Moderate Rock beat

Let

© 2008 GATEWAY CREATE PUBLISHING (BMI)
Admin. at EMICMGPUBLISHING.COM
All Rights Reserved   Used by Permission

earth and heav'nly saints pro-claim the
to the King; His saints throne tran-scends. His

pow'r and might of His great name. Let
crown and king-dom nev-er ends. Now

us ex-alt on bend-ed knee. Praise
and through-out e-ter-ni-ty, I'll

God, the ho-ly Trin-i-ty.
praise the One who died for me.

Praise God, praise God, praise God, who saved my soul. Praise God, praise God, praise God, from whom all bless-ings flow.

Praise flow. Praise

CODA
G5
3fr
flow.
mf
Praise God, from whom all bless - ings flow. Praise
Him, all crea - tures here be - low. Praise Him a - bove, ye
heav'n - ly host. Praise Fa - ther, Son and Ho - ly Ghost.
D5
5fr
G5
3fr

A NEW HALLELUJAH

Words and Music by PAUL BALOCHE,
MICHAEL W. SMITH and DEBBIE SMITH

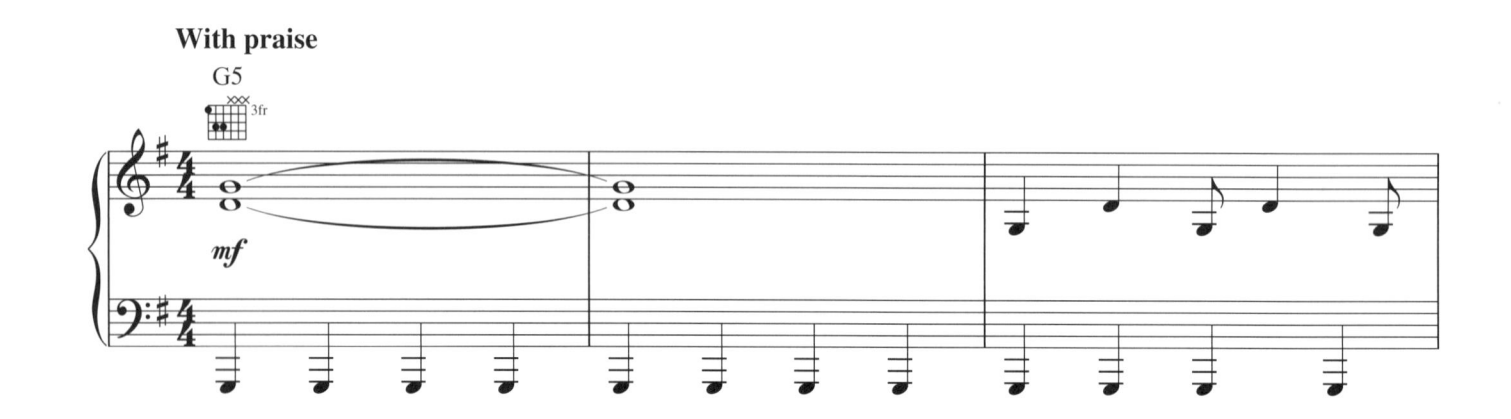

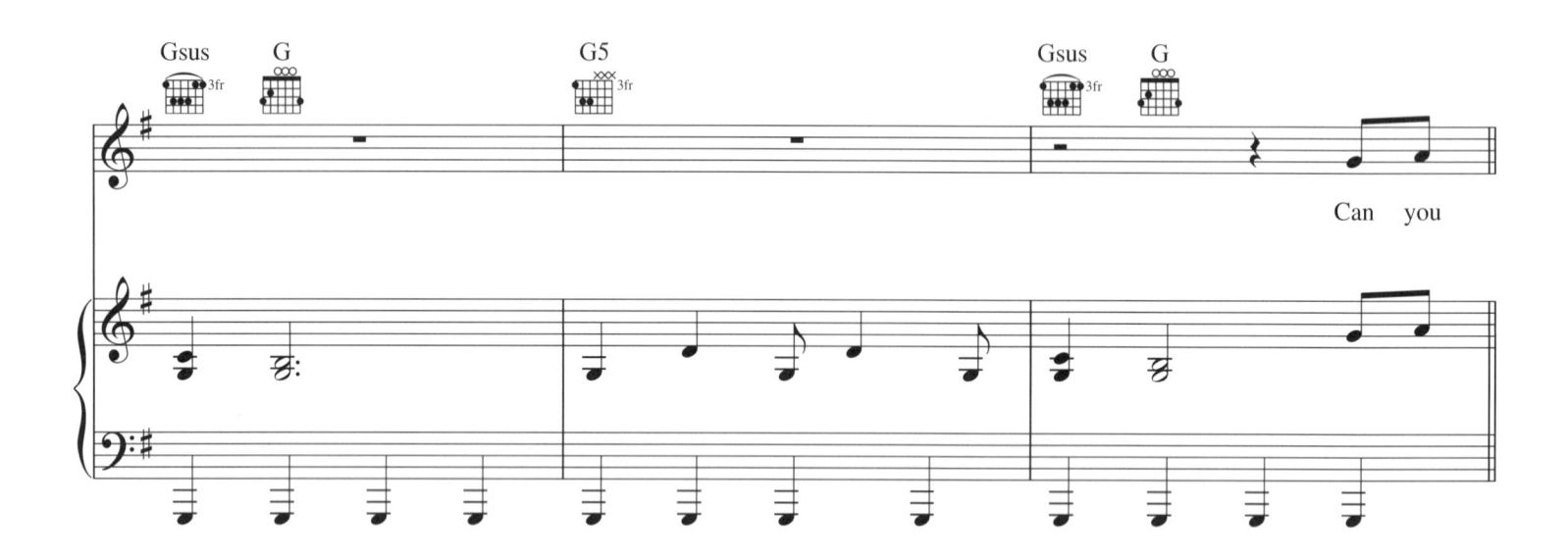

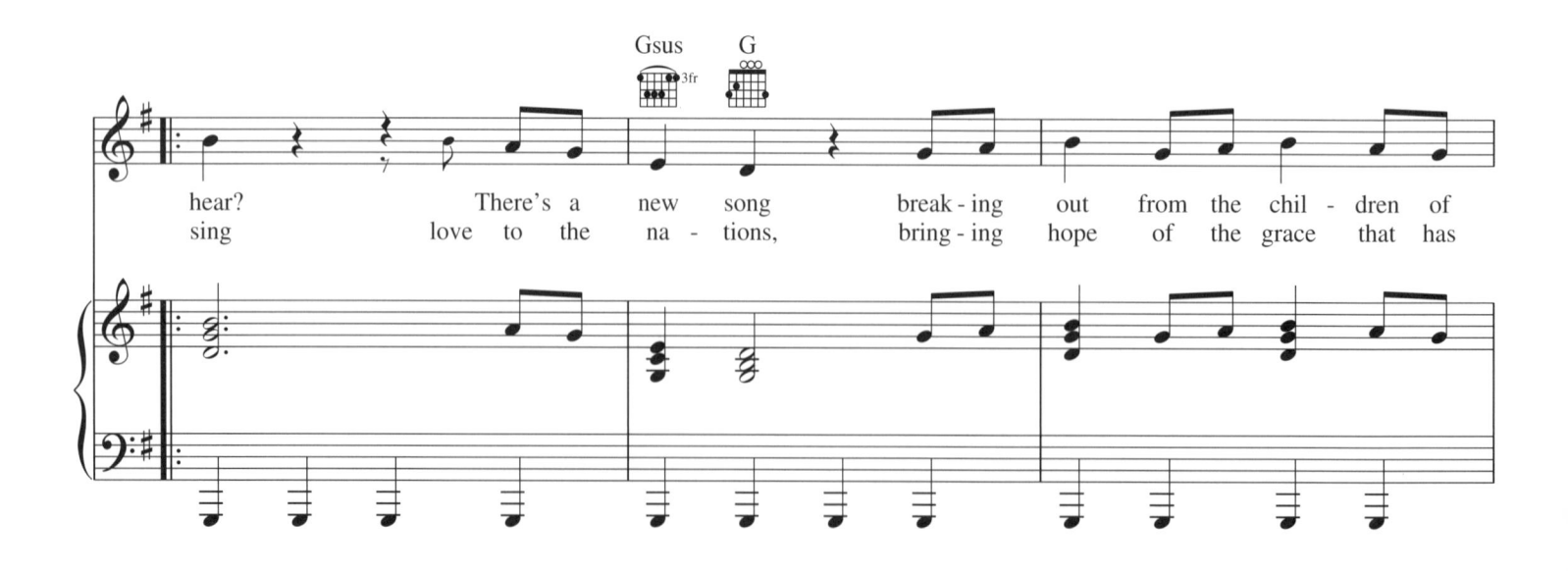

With praise

Can you hear? There's a new song, break-ing out from the chil-dren of
sing love to the na - tions, bring-ing hope of the grace that has

© 2008 INTEGRITY'S HOSANNA! MUSIC (ASCAP), LEADWORSHIP SONGS (ASCAP), WORD MUSIC, LLC (ASCAP), SMITTYFLY MUSIC (ASCAP) and THIS IS YOUR TIME MUSIC (ASCAP)
INTEGRITY'S HOSANNA! MUSIC and LEADWORSHIP SONGS Admin. at EMICMGPUBLISHING.COM
SMITTYFLY MUSIC Admin. by WORD MUSIC, LLC
All Rights Reserved   Used by Permission

177

reach to the oth-er side.

A - live, come a - live; let the song a - rise.

To Coda

Af - ri -

ca sings a new song, reaching out with a new hallelujah. Ev'ry son and ev'ry daughter, ev'ryone sing a new hallelujah.

D.S. al Coda

Arise,

180

Arise, let the church arise.

Let love reach to the other side.

Alive,

C
come a - live;
let the song a - rise.
G
Gsus
G
G5
Gsus
G
Ev - 'ry - one sing a new hal - le -
Gsus
G
Csus2
G
lu - jah. Ev - 'ry - one sing a new hal - le - lu - jah.
3fr

OPEN UP THE SKY

Words and Music by
JONATHAN STOCKSTILL

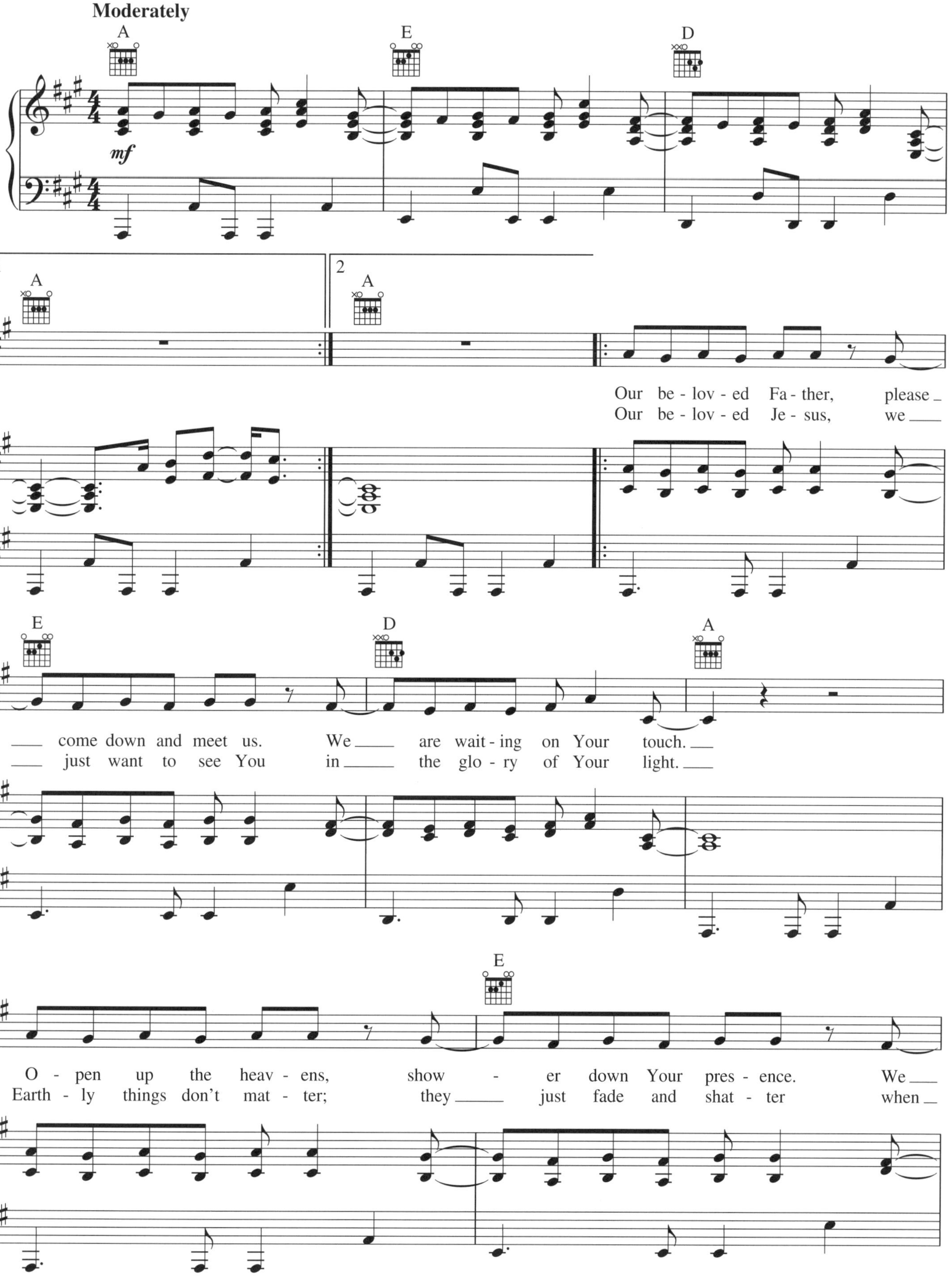

re - spond to Your great love.
we're touched by love di - vine. We won't be sat - is - fied with

an - y - thing or - di - nar - y; we won't be sat - is - fied at all.

O - pen up the sky, fall down like rain. We don't want bless-

-ings, we want You. O - pen up the sky, fall down like fire.

A
To Coda
1
E
D
A
We don't want an - y - thing but You.
E
D
A
2
E
D
D.S. al Coda
- y - thing but You.
CODA
E
D
A
- y - thing but You,
mf
E
D
A
an - y - thing but You, God.

Here we go. Let's go to the throne, the place that we be-long,

right in-to His arms.

Here we go. Let's go to the throne, the place that we be-long,

right in-to His arms.

3
A D E
mp
We won't be sat - is - fied with an - y - thing or - di - nar - y;
D
1, 2
E
3
E
we won't be sat - is - fied at all.
all.
A D A
mp – f
O - pen up the sky, fall down like rain. We don't want bless -
E D A D
- ings, we want You. O - pen up the sky, fall down like fire.

We don't want an-y-thing but You. ___ -y-thing but You. ___

Earth-ly things don't mat-ter; they ___ just fade and shat-ter when ___ we're touched by love di-vine. ___

We won't be sat-is-fied with an-y-thing or-di-nar-y;

1–3
4
D
E
E
we won't be sat - is - fied at all.
all.
A
D
A
O - pen up the sky, fall down like rain.
We don't want bless -
E
D
A
D
- ings, we want You.
O - pen up the sky, fall down like fire.
A
E
D
A
We don't want an - y - thing but You.
rit.

OUR GOD SAVES

Words and Music by PAUL BALOCHE
and BRENTON BROWN

With strength

In the name of the Father, in the name of the Son, in the name of the Spirit, Lord, we come. We're gathered to-

© 2007 INTEGRITY'S HOSANNA! MUSIC (ASCAP), LEADWORSHIP SONGS (ASCAP) and THANKYOU MUSIC (PRS)
INTEGRITY'S HOSANNA! MUSIC and LEADWORSHIP SONGS Admin. at EMICMGPUBLISHING.COM
THANKYOU MUSIC Admin. Worldwide at EMICMGPUBLISHING.COM excluding Europe which is Admin. by Kingswaysongs
All Rights Reserved   Used by Permission

191

saints bow down, as Your people sing. We will rise with You, lift-ed on Your wings, and the world will see that our God saves, our God saves.

There is hope in Your

G
To Coda
D.S. al Coda
(take 2nd ending)
name.
In the name of the
CODA
D
Mourn - ing turns
to songs of
A
Bm7
praise.
Our God saves,
G
our God saves.
Yeah.

Hear the joy-ful ___ sound ___ of our of-fer - ing, ___ as Your

195

196

PROMISES

Words and Music by
JARED ANDERSON

Up-tempo Rock

All of Your prom-is-es won't let go of me.

(All of Your prom-is-es won't let go of me.)

I've sur-ren-dered my life to Your ways,

© 2006 VERTICAL WORSHIP SONGS (ASCAP)
Admin. at EMICMGPUBLISHING.COM
All Rights Reserved   Used by Permission

and I have learned what it means to o-bey.

Je-sus, my heart has been changed by You.

I am walk-ing the path You have made, and I am seek-ing the truth

_____ ev-'ry day. _____ Je-sus, my heart _____ has been changed _____ by _____ You.

I could-n't walk a-way _____ if I tried, _____ 'cause Your love is bet-ter than life. The sun's _____ shin-ing bright _____ and it just _____ won't set, _____ 'cause Your love _____

Bm7 G D
is a - live and it lights my step. My heart is a - mazed ev - 'ry day
A Bm7 G
to the next. Your joy o - ver - takes and I can't for - get a - bout it.
D D/F♯ A Bm7
Oh, oh, oh, I can't
G D D/F♯ A
for - get a - bout it. Oh, oh,

oh, ___ I can't ___ for - get a - bout it.

Sing - ing, all of Your prom - is - es won't let go ___ of me.

D
G
A
1
D
Sing- ing, all of Your prom - is - es
(All of Your prom - is - es won't let go of me.)
G
A
D
G
A
won't let go of me.
Sing- ing,
(All of Your prom - is - es won't let go of me.)
2
D
Em7
all of Your prom - is - es won't let go of me.
D/F♯
G
D.S. al Coda
(All of Your prom - is - es won't let go of me.)
Now the sun's

CODA
G
D
D/F♯
forget about it.
Singing, all of Your promises
A
Bm7
G
won't let go of me. (All of Your promises won't let go of me.)
D
D/F♯
A
1
Bm7
All of Your promises won't let go of me. (All of Your promises
G
2
Bm7
N.C.
Yeah, I'm singing, (All of Your promises won't let go of me.)
won't let go of me.)

OVERCOME

Words and Music by
JON EGAN

Slowly, in 2

*Recorded a half step lower.

Seated above, enthroned in the Father's

© 2007 VERTICAL WORSHIP SONGS (ASCAP)
Admin. at EMICMGPUBLISHING.COM
All Rights Reserved   Used by Permission

love. Des - tined to die,
poured out for all man - kind.

God's on - ly Son, per - fect and spot - less One.
Pow - er in hand, speak - ing the Fa - ther's plan.

He nev - er sinned, but suf - fered as if He
Send - ing us out, a light in this bro - ken

did.
land. All au-thor-i-ty, ev-'ry vic-to-ry is Yours. All au-thor-i-ty, ev-'ry vic-to-ry is

C
Yours.
cresc.
Sav - ior, wor - thy of hon - or and
mf – f
Am
G
glo - ry, wor - thy of all our praise,
F
C
for You o - ver - came.

Je-sus, awe-some in pow-er for-ev-er; awe-some and great is Your name, for You o-ver-came.

for You o - ver - came.

We will o - ver - come by the blood

Am
C/G
F
of the Lamb and the word of our tes - ti - mo - ny. Ev - 'ry -
C
G
1–3
- one, o - ver - come.
4
C
Sav - ior, wor - thy of hon - or and
f
Am
G
glo - ry, wor - thy of all our praise,

for You o-ver-came.

Je-sus, awe-some in pow-er for-ev-er; awe-some and great is Your name, for You o-ver-came.

READY NOW

Words and Music by
JARED ANDERSON

Moderately

Come like You prom-ised You would. I want to sur-ren-
I feel like a blind man in Your sight. I know that I'm wick-
-der for good. I know that I need
-ed in Your eyes. So wash me and make

© 2006 VERTICAL WORSHIP SONGS (ASCAP)
Admin. at EMICMGPUBLISHING.COM
All Rights Reserved Used by Permission

213

Lyrics:
I lift them high. They're Yours, not mine, to do, do what You will, do what You will, do what You will.

I'm ready now,
I'm ready now, I'm ready now.
Do what You will. I'm ready now,
I'm ready now, I'm ready now.

216

| D | Em |

Do what You will. I'm read-y now,

| Cmaj7 | G |

I'm read-y now, I'm read-y now.

| A | Em |

Do what You will. I'm read-y now,

| Cmaj7 | G |

I'm read-y now, I'm read-y now.

D
N.C.
mp
G
Take my heart
A7
C
and make it new,
sim.
make it true,
D
G
(My
make it like You.
Take my hands,

218

219

REVELATION SONG

Words and Music by
JENNIE LEE RIDDLE

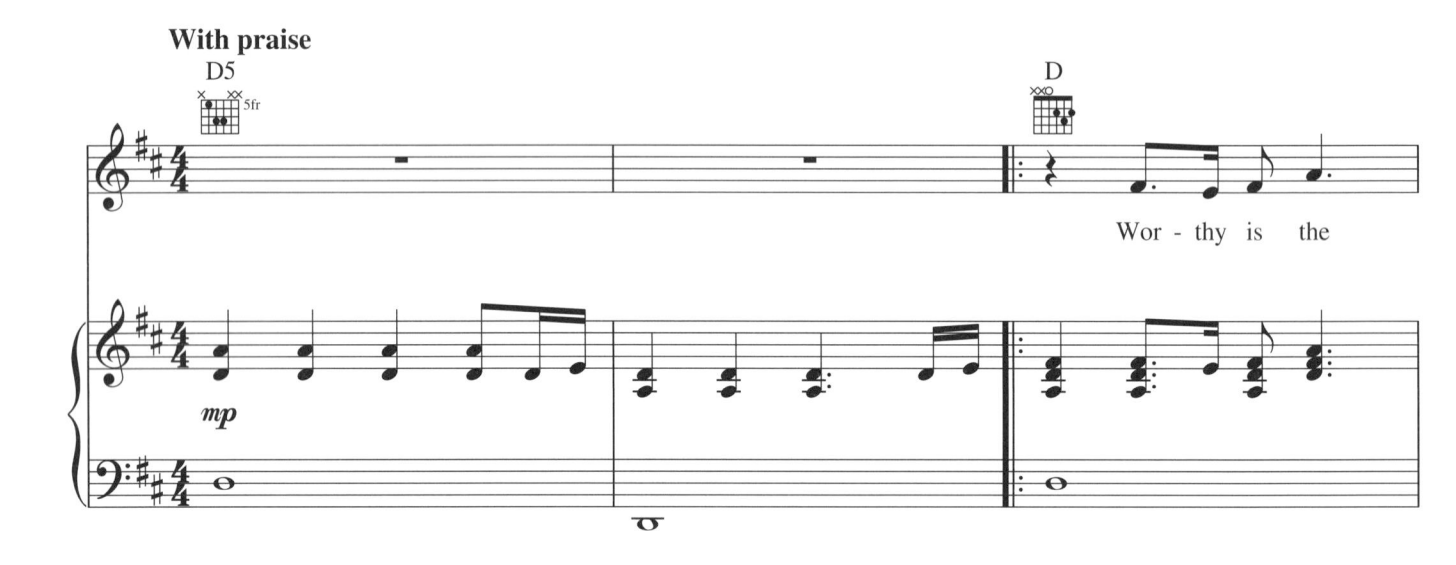

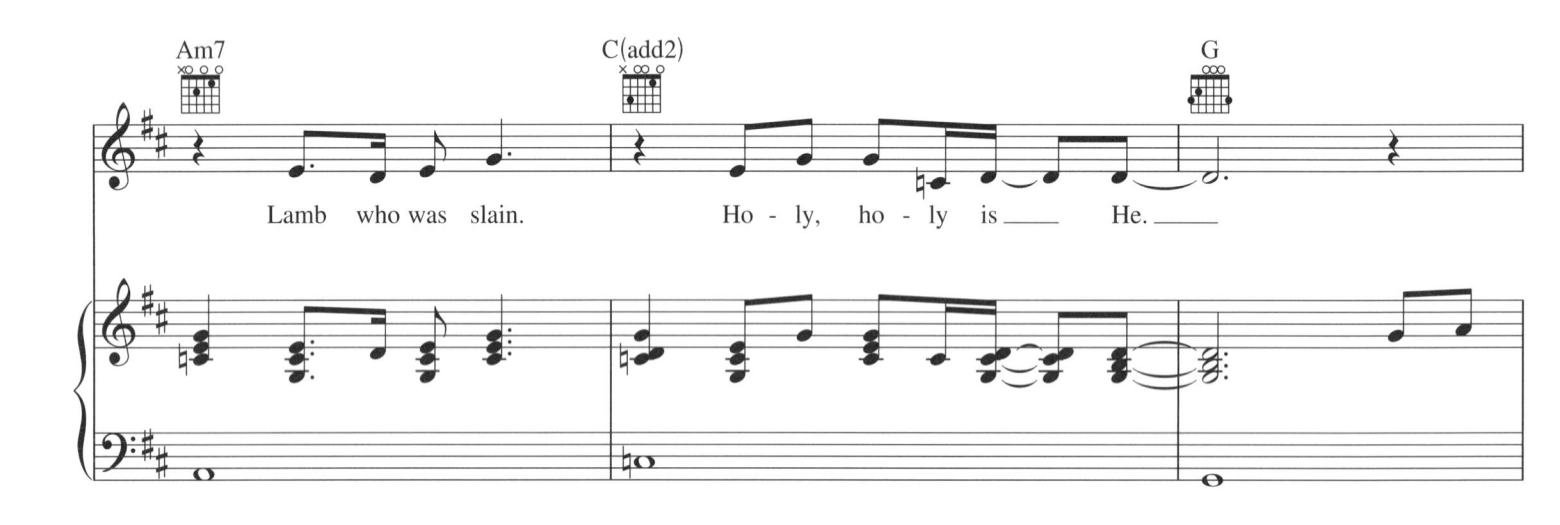

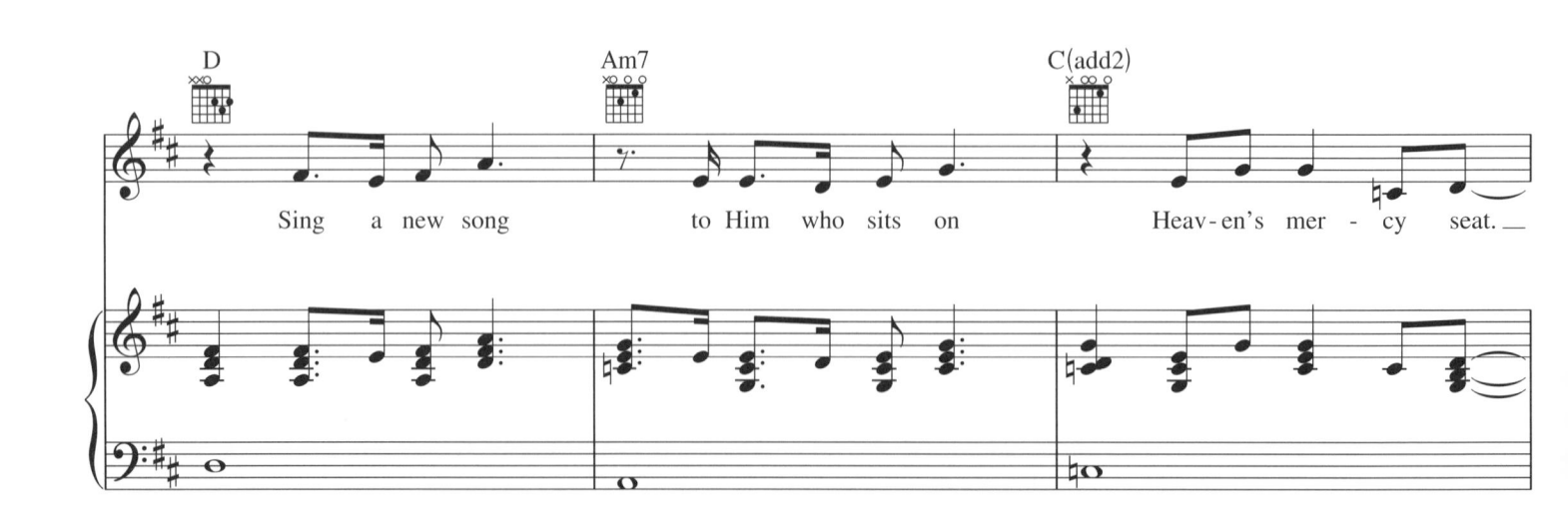

With praise

Wor-thy is the Lamb who was slain. Ho-ly, ho-ly is He.

Sing a new song to Him who sits on Heav-en's mer-cy seat.

© 2004 GATEWAY CREATE PUBLISHING (BMI)
Admin. at EMICMGPUBLISHING.COM
All Rights Reserved   Used by Permission

Ho-ly, ho-ly, ho-ly is the Lord God Al-might-y, who was and is and is to come. With all cre-a-tion I sing praise to the King of kings. You are my ev-'ry-thing, and

I will adore You.

I will adore You. Clothed in rainbows of living color, flashes of lightning, rolls of thunder. Blessing and honor, strength and

223

awe-struck won-der, at the men-tion of Your name.

Je-sus, Your name is pow-er,

breath and liv-ing wa-ter, such a mar-v'lous mys-

-ter-y. Ho-ly, ho-ly, ho-ly

Am7
C
is the Lord God Al-might - y, who was and is and is to come.
G
D
With all cre - a - tion I sing
Am7
G/B
C
praise to the King of kings. You are my ev - 'ry - thing, and
1, 2
G
3
G
D
I will a - dore You. I will a - dore You.
rit.

RISING

Words and Music by PAUL BALOCHE
and MATT REDMAN

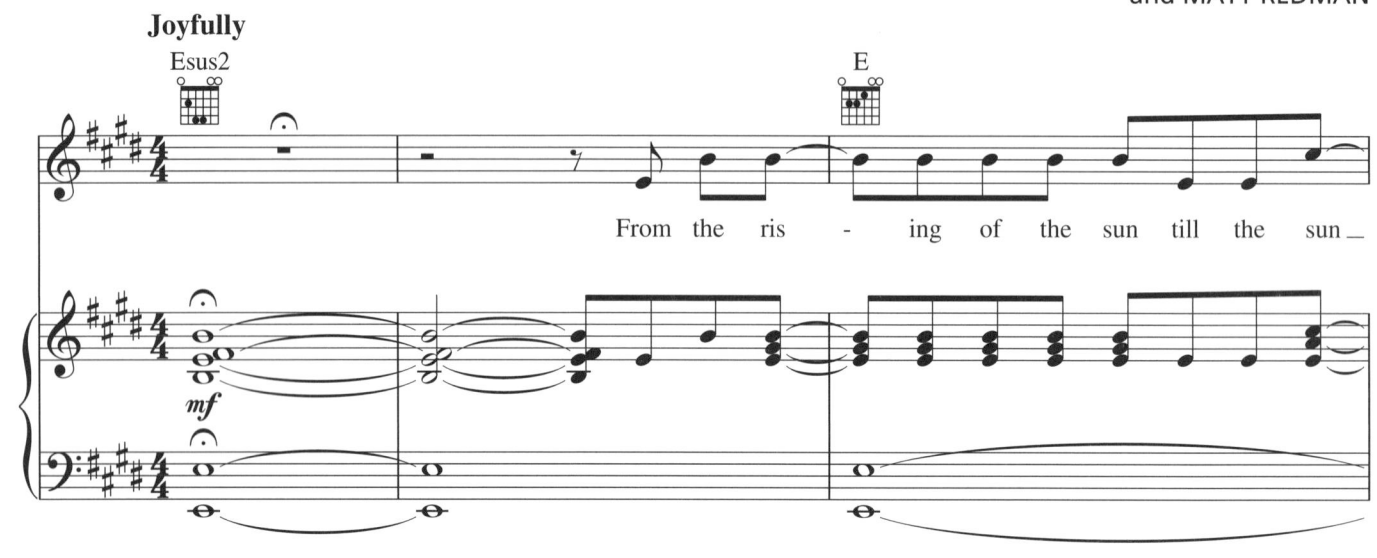

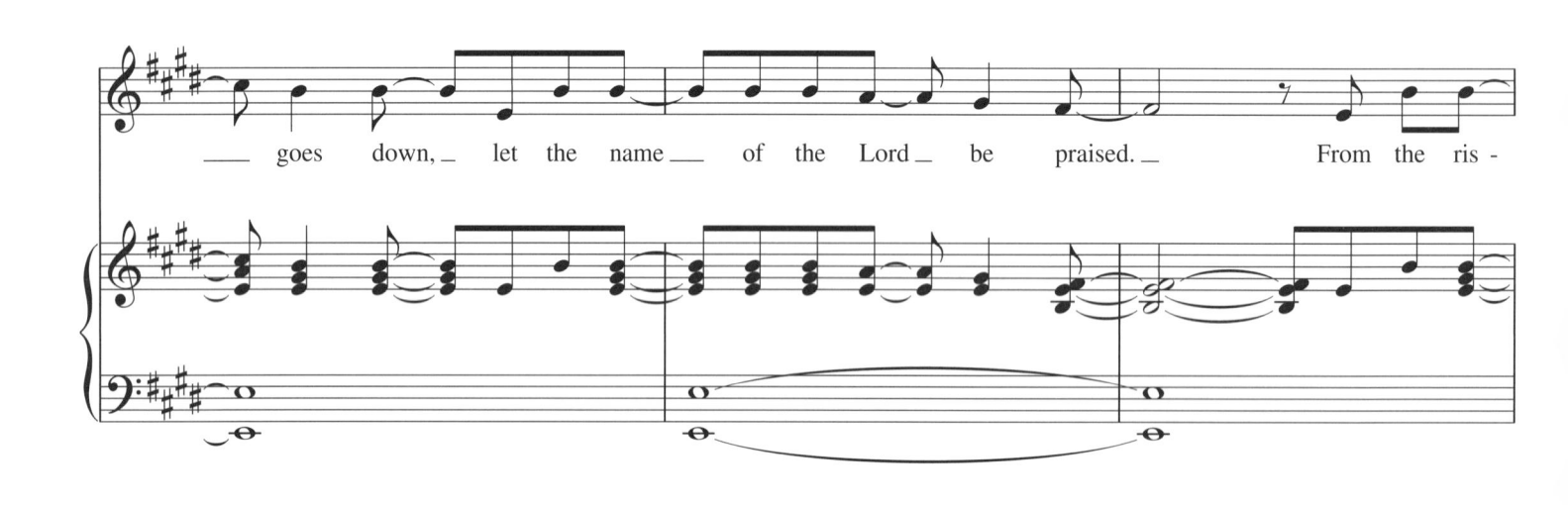

Joyfully

From the rising of the sun till the sun goes down, let the name of the Lord be praised. From the rising of the sun till the sun goes down, let the name of the Lord be praised.

© 2006 INTEGRITY'S HOSANNA! MUSIC (ASCAP) and THANKYOU MUSIC (PRS)
INTEGRITY'S HOSANNA! MUSIC Admin. at EMICMGPUBLISHING.COM
THANKYOU MUSIC Admin. Worldwide at EMICMGPUBLISHING.COM excluding Europe which is Admin. by Kingswaysongs
All Rights Reserved   Used by Permission

We're gathered to worship, becoming a choir to sing Your praise, lifting our voices, joining our hearts in this house today.

We're gather to go out; to cities and towns, we'll take Your name into the nations, shining Your light in the darkest place. People of God,

Asus2(♯4)
A
Asus2(♯4)
A
in the pow - er of God,
for the
king - dom of God
we sing.
we live.
𝄋 E
From the ris - ing of the sun till the sun
B/D♯
E
B/D♯
goes down, let the name of the Lord be praised.
From the ris -
E
B/D♯
E
- ing of the sun till the sun goes down, let the name of the Lord be praised.
4fr

229

Guitar solo ad lib.

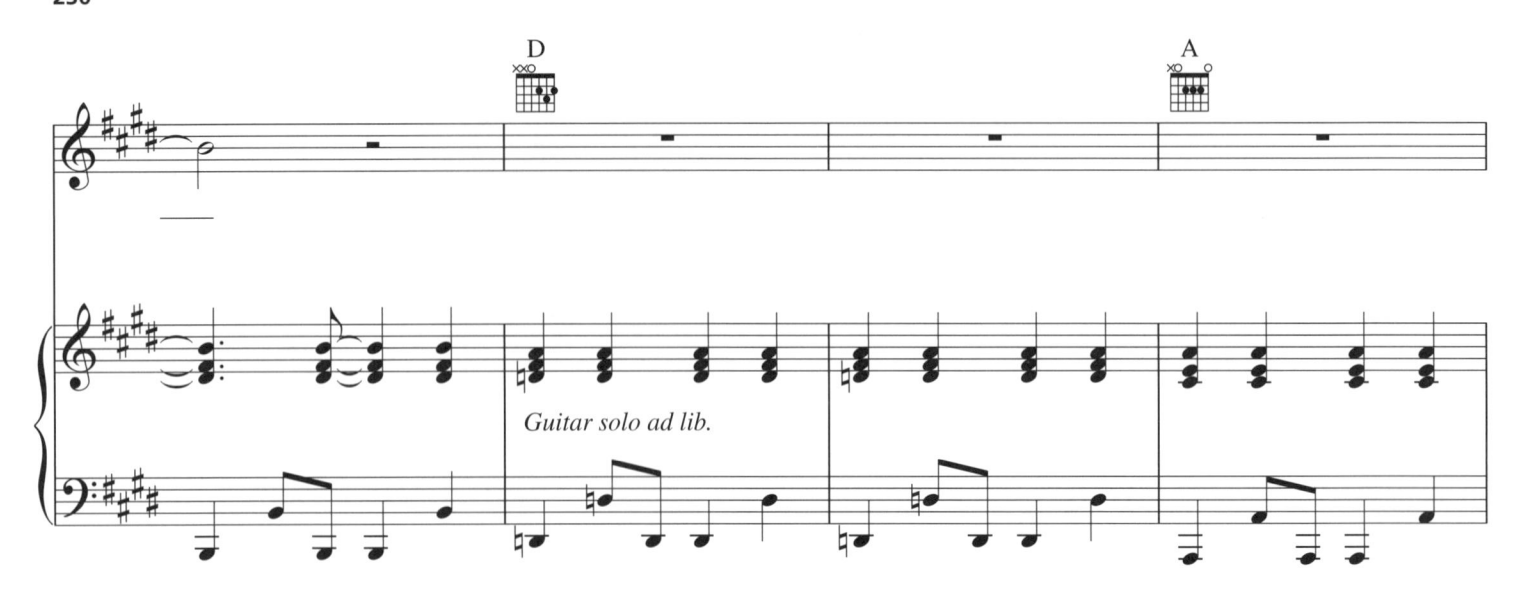

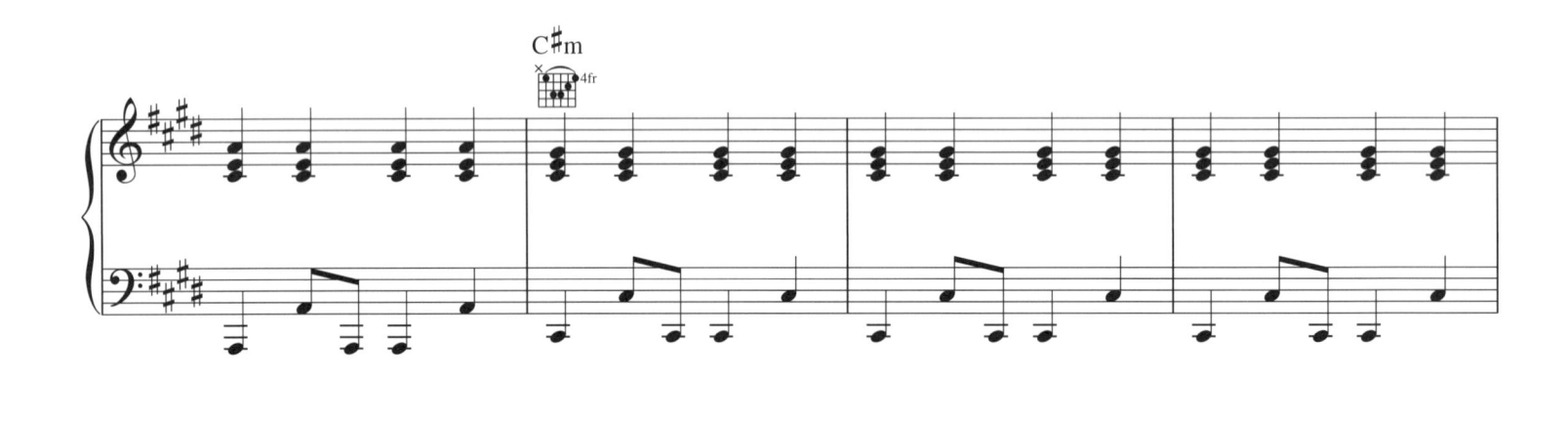

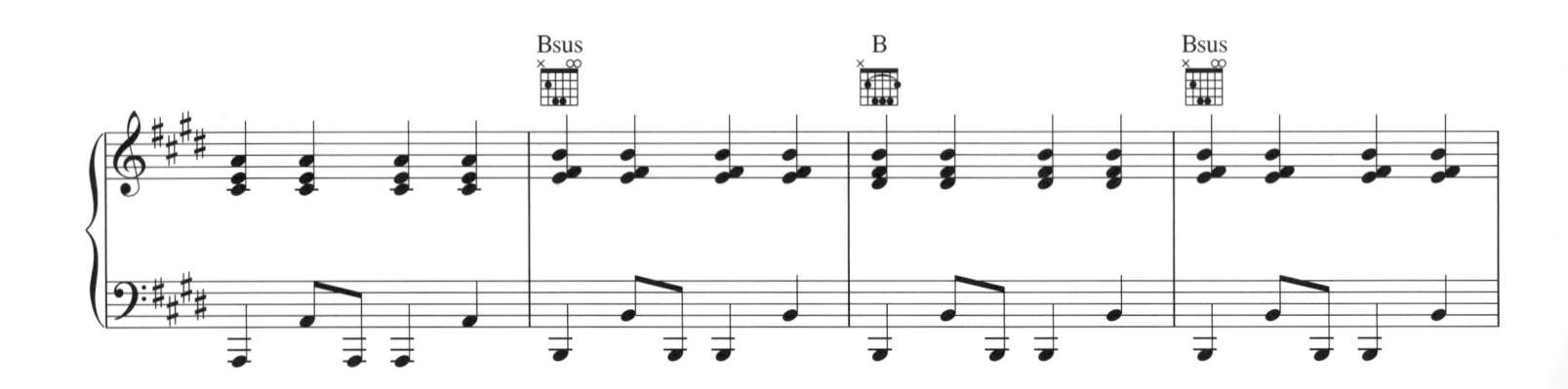

From the ris-ing of the sun till the sun goes down, let the name of the Lord be praised. From the ris-ing of the sun till the sun goes down, let the name of the Lord be praised. From the sky to the depths, from the east to the west, from the ris-

D.S. al Coda

232

CODA

We give You praise.

Lord, we give You praise. We give You praise.

From the ris-ing of the sun till the sun goes down, let the name of the Lord be praised.

STAY AMAZED

Words and Music by KLAUS KUEHN,
JAMIE BIRKENFELD and ROBERT QUINTANA

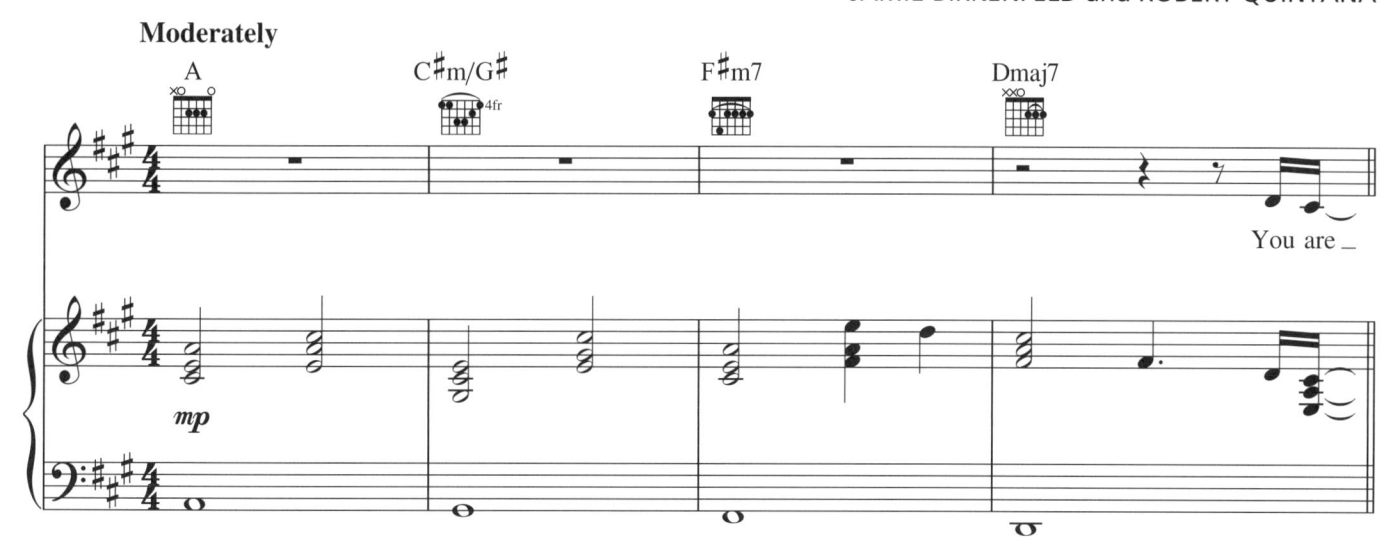

Moderately

You are en-throned a-bove the heav-ens. The earth and all cre-a-tion bow be-fore You. You are crowned with strength and glo-

© 2007 GATEWAY CREATE PUBLISHING (BMI)
Admin. at EMICMGPUBLISHING.COM
All Rights Reserved Used by Permission

Dmaj7
A
E
- ry. The an - gels cry - ing, "Ho - ly" all sur - round You. For -
F♯m7
D
A/C♯
ev - er You will stand. Your king - dom has no end.
D
E
A
E/G♯
O Ho - ly God, I stay a - mazed. You are
mf–f
F♯m7
D
E
so much more than words could ev - er say. O Ho - ly God,

I pour out my praise on the One who nev-er ceas-es to a-maze. You are lov-ing be-yond meas-ure. Your pres-ence is the treas-ure I am seek-ing. You are an all-con-sum-ing fi-re, and I am Your de-si-re, and You are mine. For-ev-er, for-ev - er __ You _ will stand. _____ Your king - dom _ has _ no end. __

D.S. al Coda

___ O Ho - ly God, _

CODA

maze. I'm pour - ing out

my praise _ on You. I'm pour - ing out my love _ on You.

I'm pour - ing out my praise _ on You. I'm pour - ing out

237

THANK YOU, LORD

Words and Music by PAUL BALOCHE
and DON MOEN

Moderately

I come be-fore You to-day,
For all You've done in my life;

and there's just one thing that I want to say:
You took my dark-ness and gave me Your light.

© 2004 INTEGRITY'S HOSANNA! MUSIC (ASCAP)
Admin. at EMICMGPUBLISHING.COM
All Rights Reserved   Used by Permission

Thank You, Lord. ___ Thank You, Lord. ___
Thank You, Lord. ___ Thank You, Lord. ___

For all You've giv-en to me, ___
You took my sin and my shame, ___

for all the bless-ings that I ___ can-not see, ___
You took my sick-ness and healed ___ all my pain. ___

thank You, Lord. ___ Thank You, Lord. ___
Thank You, Lord. ___ Thank You, Lord. ___

With a grateful heart, with a song of praise, with an out-stretched arm, I will bless Your name.

Thank You, Lord. I just want to thank You, Lord.

Thank You, Lord. I just want to thank You, Lord.

Thank You, Lord.

Thank You, Lord.

Vocal ad lib.

F C Gm7 Dm
Bb C Bb C
Thank You, Lord.
Thank You, Lord.
F C Gm7
Dm C/D Dm Bb C
Thank You, Lord.

Thank You, Lord. With a grateful heart, with a song of praise, with an out-stretched arm, I will bless Your name. Oh, Thank You, Lord. I just want to thank You, Lord.

Thank You, Lord. I just want to thank You, Lord. Thank You, Lord. Thank You, Lord. Thank You, Lord.

TODAY
(As for Me and My House)

Words and Music by BRIAN DOERKSEN
and SANDRA GAGE

*Recorded a half step higher.

© 2003 INTEGRITY'S HOSANNA! MUSIC (ASCAP)
Admin. at EMICMGPUBLISHING.com
All Rights Reserved Used by Permission

A♭/C D♭ A♭ A♭/G
3fr 4fr
to give my "yes" to You. To - day I choose
A♭/C D♭ A♭ Fm7
3fr 4fr
to hear Your voice and live. To - day I choose
A♭/E♭ A♭ E♭ B♭m
4fr 3fr
to fol - low You. And as for me and my house,
f
D♭maj7 A♭sus A♭ E♭ B♭m D♭maj7
4fr 4fr 3fr
we will serve You. As for me and my house, we will

1
A♭/E♭ E♭ A♭ A♭/G
spend our lives on You to - day, to - day.
A♭/C D♭
Oh, to - day
2
A♭/E♭ E♭
spend our lives on You, oh.
B♭m D♭maj7 A♭sus A♭
As for me and my house, we will serve You.
E♭ B♭m D♭maj7 A♭/E♭ E♭
And as for me and my house, we will spend our lives on You to -

A♭ D♭ Fm B♭m E♭
day. Won-der-ful Coun-sel-or, Ev-er-last-ing Fa-ther, E-
mp
D♭ Fm B♭m
ter-nal King, Lord of Hosts, will-ing-ly we fol-
E♭sus E♭ B♭ B♭/A B♭/D E♭
-low. To-day I choose You.
f
B♭ Gm Fsus
To-day I choose to give my "yes" to You, Lord,

to give my "yes" to You, Lord. To-day I choose to fol-low You. To-day I choose to give my "yes" to You. As for me and my house, we will serve You. As for me and my house,

| Ebmaj7 | Fsus | F | Cm |

we will spend our lives on You. As for me and my house,

| Ebmaj7 | Gm | F | Cm |

we will serve You. As for me and my house,

| Ebmaj7 | Bb | F | Cm7 |

we will spend our lives on You.

| Ebmaj7 | Gm | F | Cm7 |

We will spend our lives on You.

E♭maj7 Fsus B♭ B♭/A
3fr
We will spend our lives on You.
B♭/D E♭maj7 B♭ B♭/A
Your fame, for
mf
B♭/D E♭maj7 B♭ B♭/A B♭/D E♭maj7
Your name.
B♭ B♭/A B♭/D E♭maj7
We will spend our lives on You.

TODAY IS THE DAY

Words and Music by LINCOLN BREWSTER
and PAUL BALOCHE

Oh, oh, oh, oh, oh, oh. Oh, oh, oh, oh, oh, oh.

I'm casting my cares aside,
a - side,

I'm leaving my past behind.
I'm leaving my doubts behind.

© 2008 INTEGRITY'S PRAISE! MUSIC (BMI), INTEGRITY'S HOSANNA! MUSIC (ASCAP) and LEADWORSHIP SONGS (ASCAP)
Admin. at EMICMGPUBLISHING.COM
All Rights Reserved   Used by Permission

253

I'm set-ting my heart ___ and mind ___ on You, ___
I'm giv-ing my hopes ___ and dreams ___ to You, ___

Je - sus. ___
Je - sus. ___

I'm reach-ing my {hand ___ / hands ___} to Yours, ___ be - liev-ing there's so ___

___ much more, ___ know-ing that all ___ You have ___ in store ___

for me is good, _is good._ To-day is the day_ _You_ have made;_ I will re-joice_ and be glad_ in_ it. _To-day is the day_ _You_ have made; I will re-joice_ _and be glad_ in_ it. And I_ won't wor-ry 'bout_ _to-mor-row, I'm trust-ing in what You say._ To-day is the day.

To-day is the day.

I'm put-ting my fears

Guitar solo ad lib.

Bm7(add4)
G
D
Gsus2
D
Gsus2
D
G
I will stand up - on
D
G
Your truth. (I will stand up - on Your truth.) And all

my days I'll live for You. (All my days I'll live for You.) And I will stand upon Your truth. (I will stand upon Your truth.) And all my days I'll live for You. (All my days I'll live.) Today is the day

A/C♯
Bm7
You have made; I will re - joice and be glad in it.
G
D
A/C♯
To - day is the day You have made; I will re - joice
D/F♯
G
and be glad in it. And I
Em7
D/F♯
won't wor - ry 'bout to - mor - row; I'm giv -

259

WHAT CAN I DO?

Words and Music by PAUL BALOCHE
and GRAHAM KENDRICK

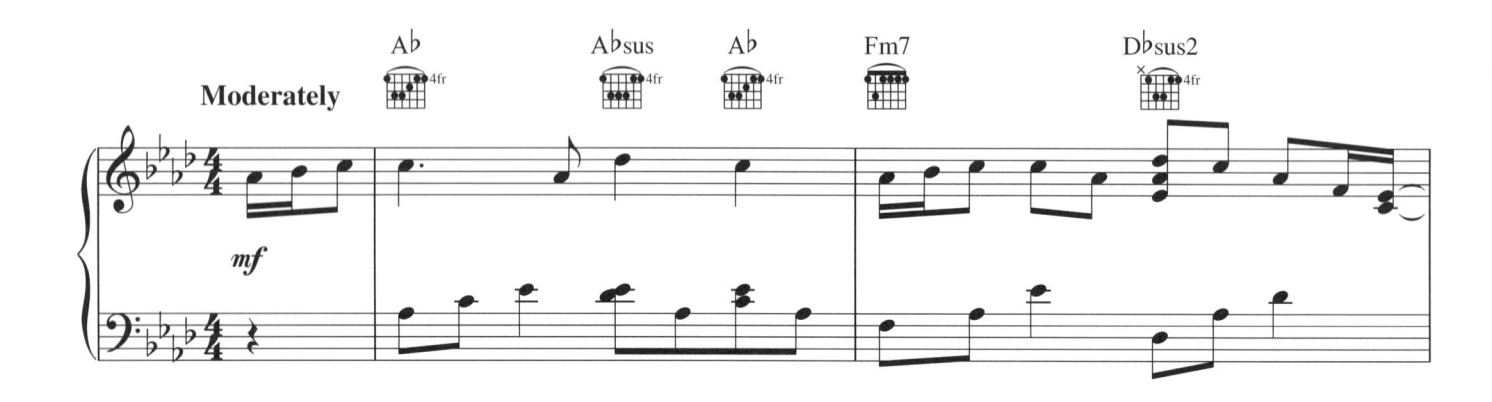

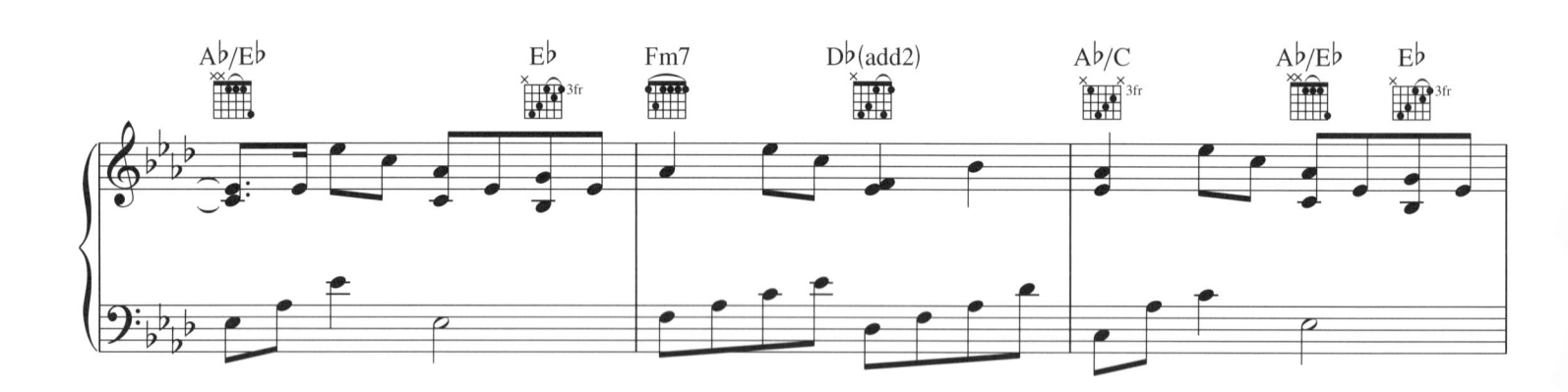

Moderately

When I see the beau-ty of a sun-set's
sto - ry of a God of

© 2006 INTEGRITY'S HOSANNA! MUSIC (ASCAP) and MAKE WAY MUSIC (PRS)
INTEGRITY'S HOSANNA! MUSIC Admin. at EMICMGPUBLISHING.COM
MAKE WAY MUSIC Admin. in the United States and Canada by MUSIC SERVICES
All Rights Reserved   Used by Permission

glory, amazing artistry across the evening
mercy who shared humanity and suffered by our

sky, when I feel the mystery of a distant
side, of the cross they nailed You to, but could not

galaxy, it awes and humbles me to be
hold You; now You're making all things new by the

loved by a God so high.
pow'r of Your risen life. What can I

do but thank You? What can I do but give my life to You? _____ Hal-le-lu-jah! Hal-le-lu-jah! What can I do but praise You ev-er-y day ___ with ev-'ry-thing I do? ___ Hal-le-lu-jah! Hal-le-lu-jah! ____ Hal-le-lu -

2
A♭ A♭/C A♭/E♭ E♭ Fm7 D♭
jah! When I hear the ___ Hal - le - lu - jah!
mf
A♭ E♭sus Fm7 D♭ A♭
E♭sus E♭ A♭ A♭sus A♭
What can I do but thank You?
dim.
mp
Fm7 D♭sus2 A♭ A♭/E♭ E♭
What can I do but give my life to You? ___ Hal - le - lu - jah!

Fm7 D♭sus2 A♭ B♭m7 A♭
Hal - le - lu - jah! What can I do but praise You
mf
Fm7 D♭ A♭ A♭/E♭ E♭
ev - er - y day with ev - 'ry - thing I do? Hal - le - lu - jah!
Fm7 D♭ A♭ D♭ A♭
Hal - le - lu - jah! What can I do but thank You?
f
Fm7 D♭ A♭ Fm/E♭ E♭
What can I do but give my life to You? Hal - le - lu - jah!
4fr
3fr

Fm7 D♭sus2 A♭ B♭m7 A♭
Hal - le - lu - jah! What can I do but praise You
Fm7 D♭ A♭ Fm/E♭ E♭
ev - er - y day with ev - 'ry - thing I do? Hal - le - lu - jah!
Fm7 D♭sus2 A♭/C A♭/E♭ E♭ A♭ D♭ A♭
Hal - le - lu - jah! Hal - le - lu - jah!
Fm7 D♭sus2 A♭ A♭/E♭ E♭ Fm7 D♭sus2 A♭
rit.

WORSHIPING YOU

Words and Music by
JONATHAN STOCKSTILL

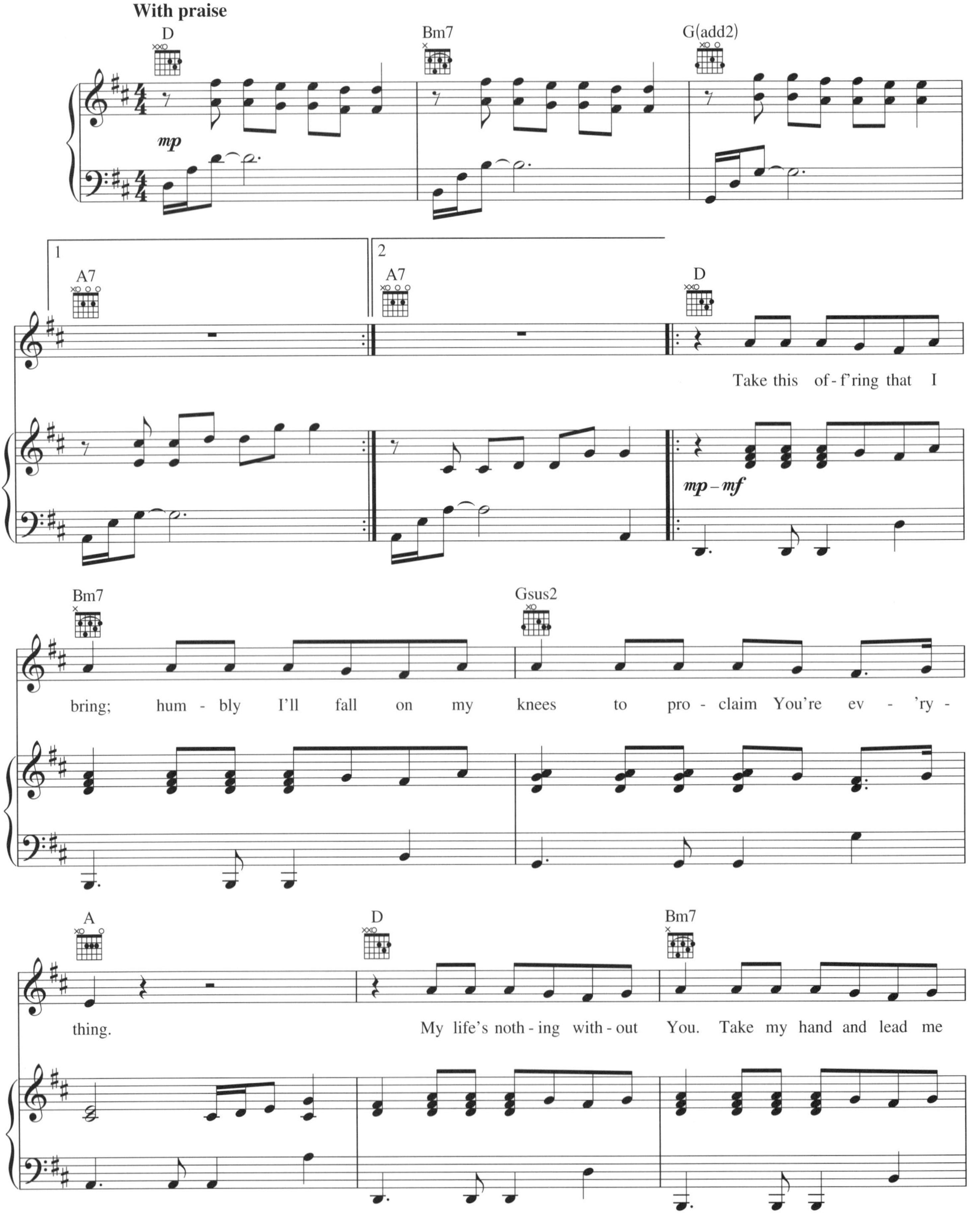

Gsus2
Asus
A
through; You are my sus - tain - ing love.
I
A/G
G
A/G
G
D
live to wor - ship You.
mf
A/G
G
A/G
G
I live to wor - ship
Bm7
G
A
D
You.
Here I am,
f

worshiping You, with all I am, worshiping You. I'm bowing down in spirit and truth, with lifted hands, worshiping You.

2
A
G
D
wor - ship - ing You.
Vocal ad lib.
mf building on repeats
Bm7
Gsus2
Repeat ad lib.
Asus
A
Last time
Asus
A
D
I'm gon - na wor - ship You for - ev - er,
mp building on repeats
Asus
Em7
I'm gon - na wor - ship You.
I'm gon - na wor - ship You for - ev - er,

Repeat ad lib. | **Last time**

Gsus2 — I'm gonna worship You. : Gsus2 — I'm gonna worship You.

D — Here I am, A — worshiping You, Em7 D/F# — with all I am,

G — worshiping You. D — I'm bowing down A — in spirit and truth,

Em7 — with lifted hands, G — worshiping You. D

YOU ARE FOR ME

Words and Music by
KARI JOBE

Gently flowing

So faithful, so constant, so loving and so true, so powerful in all You do. You fill me, You see

© 2008 GATEWAY CREATE PUBLISHING (BMI)
Admin. at EMICMGPUBLISHING.COM
All Rights Reserved   Used by Permission

me, You know my ev-'ry move. You love for me to sing to You. I know that You are for me. I know that You are for me. I know that You will never forsake me in my weakness. And I know that You have come now, e-

-ven if ___ to write ___ up-on my heart, ___ to re-mind me ___ who You are. ___

So pa - tient, so gra -

F/A
Gm7
E♭
3fr
-cious, so mer - ci-ful and true, so won - der-ful in all You do. You
B♭
F/A
Gm7
fill me, You see me, You know my ev - 'ry move. You love
E♭
3fr
D.S. al Coda
for me to sing to You. Lord, I know
CODA
Gm7
E♭
3fr
to re - mind me. Lord, I know

B♭
F/A
— that You — are for — me, I know — that You — are for — me. I know —
mf
Gm7
E♭
3fr
— that You — will nev - er for - sake — me in — my weak - ness. And — I know —
B♭
F/A
— that You — have come — now, e - ven if — to write — up - on my
Gm7
E♭
3fr
heart, to re - mind — me who — You — are. —
mp

276

To _____ re - mind _ me. _____

I know _

...that You are for me, I know that You are for me. I know that You will never forsake me in my weakness. And I know that You have come now, even if to write upon my heart, to remind me who You are.

YOU ARE GOD ALONE
(not a god)

Words and Music by BILLY J. FOOTE
and CINDY FOOTE

*Recorded a half step lower.

© 2004 INTEGRITY'S HOSANNA! MUSIC (ASCAP) and BILLY FOOTE SONGS (ASCAP)
Admin. at EMICMGPUBLISHING.COM
All Rights Reserved   Used by Permission

D
Dsus
You are not a god de - pend - ent on
A/D
an - y mor - tal man. You are not a god in need
Bm
G
D
of an - y - thing we can give. By Your
A/D
Dsus
plan, that's just the way it is.

You are not a / You're the on-ly
god creat-ed by human hands. / God whose pow-er none can con-tend.
You are not a god depend-ent on / You're the on-ly God whose name and
an-y mor-tal man. You are not a god in need / praise will nev-er end. You're the on-ly God who's wor-

Bm
G
D
of anything we can give. By Your
thy of ev-'ry-thing we can give. You are
A/C♯
D/F♯
Gsus2
plan, that's just the way it is.
God, that's just the way it is.
D
You are God alone. From be-
A/C♯
fore time began, You were on Your throne.

Bm
G
You are God a - lone.
D
And right now, in the good times and bad,
A/C♯
Bm
You are on Your throne, and
G
You are God a - lone.
1

Un - change - a - ble, ___ un - shak - a - ble, ___ un - stop - pa - ble, ___ that's what You are. ___ Un - change - a - ble, ___ un - shak - a - ble, ___

un-stop-pa-ble, that's what You are.

You are God alone. From be-fore time be-gan, You were on Your throne.

You are God alone.

Right now, in the good times and bad, You are on Your throne, and You are God alone. Unchange- -able, unshak - able, un - stop - pa - ble, that's what You are.

Repeat and Fade | **Optional Ending**

YOU ARE THE ONE

Words and Music by PAUL BALOCHE
and LINCOLN BREWSTER

Moderately

You're the One who made the heav-ens, You're the One who shaped the earth. You're the One who formed my heart long be-fore my birth. I be-

© 2002 INTEGRITY'S HOSANNA! MUSIC (ASCAP) and INTEGRITY'S PRAISE! MUSIC (BMI)
Admin. at EMICMGPUBLISHING.COM
All Rights Reserved Used by Permission

288

-lieve You'll always lead me, all my days have been ordained. All Your thoughts t'ward me are holy, full of love and grace. You are the One, You are holy. You are the One, You are worthy.

You are the One, _ You _ are the One _ ev-er-last - ing. _

You are the One _ I will wor - ship, You are the One _ I will serve _

_ all my days. _ You are the One, _ You _ are the One _ ev-er-last -

- ing. _ You are the One. _

Bsus
E/G♯
Asus2
1
Bsus
Je - sus, You're the One.
You're the
2
Bsus
F♯m7
E
A/E
E
F♯m7
A
D.S. al Coda
CODA
Asus2
E/G♯
Asus2
Bsus
You are the One.
(Lead vocal ad lib.)
You are the One.

291

You are the One.

You are the One.

You are the One.

You are the One.

Repeat ad lib.

You are the One.

Final Ending

You are the One.

rit.

YOU ARE GOOD

Words and Music by
KARI JOBE

Your kindness leads me to repentance. Your goodness draws me to Your side. Your mercy calls me to be like You. Your

© 2008 GATEWAY CREATE PUBLISHING (BMI)
Admin. at EMICMGPUBLISHING.COM
All Rights Reserved Used by Permission

fa - vor is my de - light. Ev - er - y day I'll a-

wak - en my praise, and pour out a song from my heart.

You are good, You are good, You are good,

and Your mer - cy is for - ev - er. You are

Lyrics:
good, You are good, You are good, and Your mercy is forever. You alone are good. We worship You, oh, yeah. Your kind-

-ness ___ leads me to ___ re - pen - tance. ___ Your good-

-ness ___ draws ___ me to ___ Your side. ___ Your mer-

-cy ___ calls me to ___ be like ___ You, ___ and ___ Your fa-

-vor is ___ my de - light. ___ Ev - er - y ___ day ___ I'll awaken my praise, and pour out a song from my heart. You are good, You are good, (Vocal ad lib. on repeats) You are good, and Your mercy is forever. You are good, You are good,

E/G#
F#m7
You are good, and Your mer - cy is for -
1, 2
D
A/E
E
3
ev - er. You are good, ev - er. Your kind -
dim.
A
E/G#
- ness is for - ev - er, Your good - ness is for - ev - er, Your mer -
mp
F#m7
Repeat ad lib.
D
Final Ending
- cy is for - ev - er, for - ev - er. Your kind - ev - er.

YOU GAVE YOUR LIFE AWAY

Words and Music by PAUL BALOCHE
and KATHRYN SCOTT

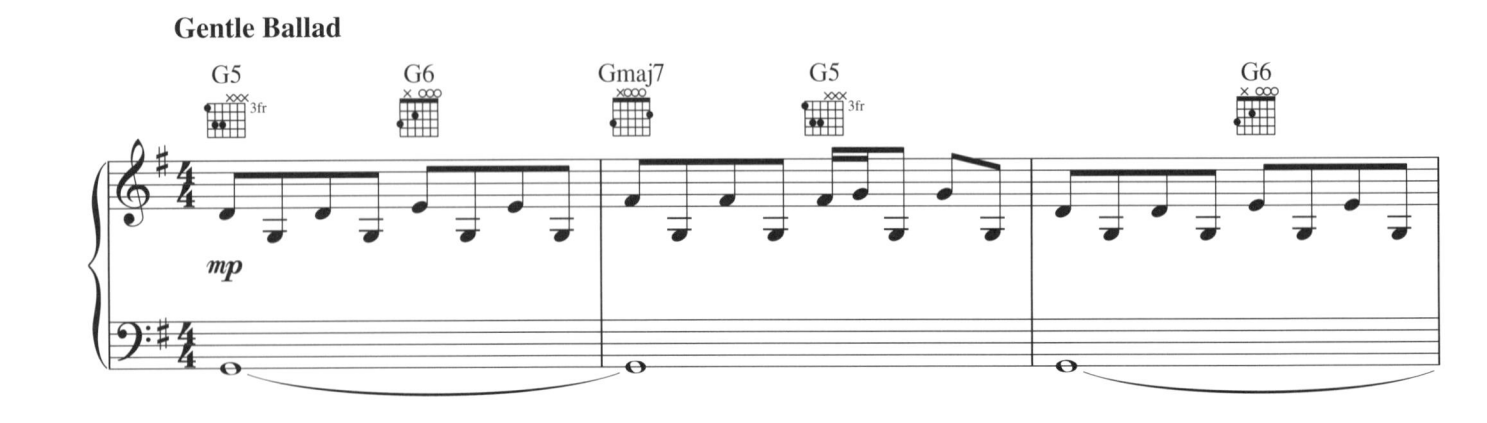

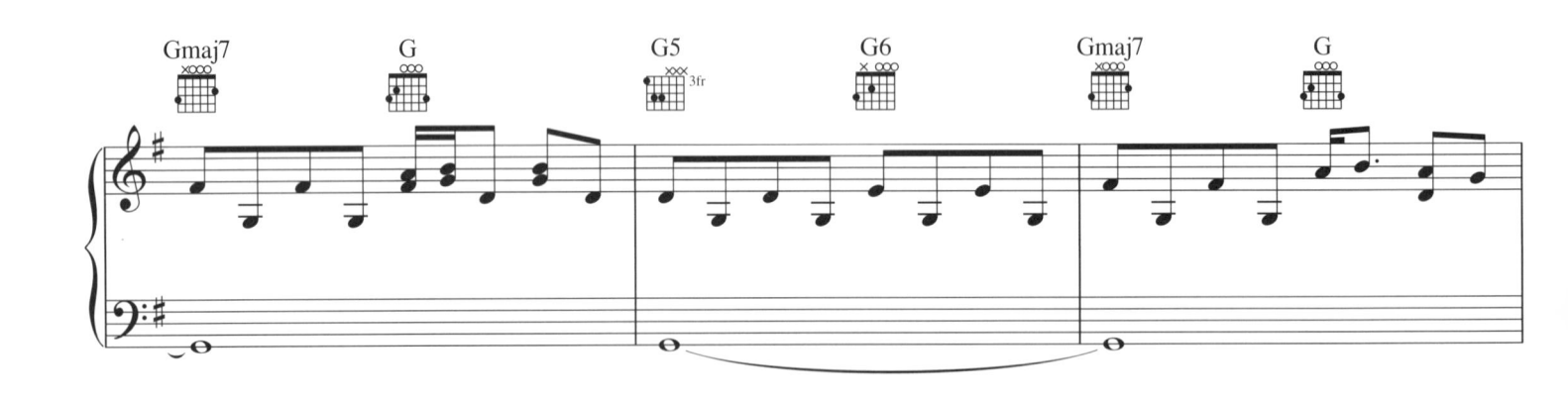

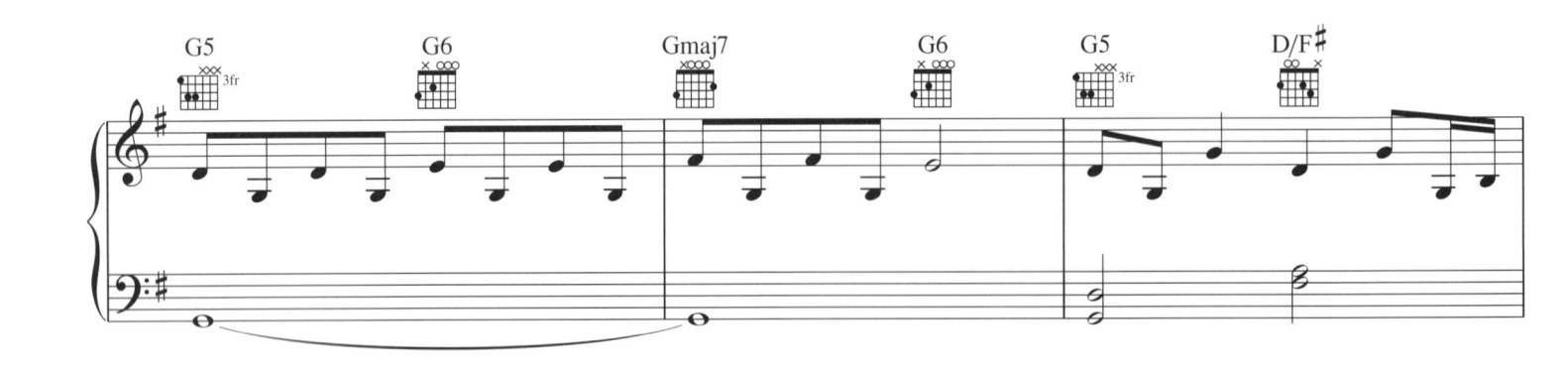

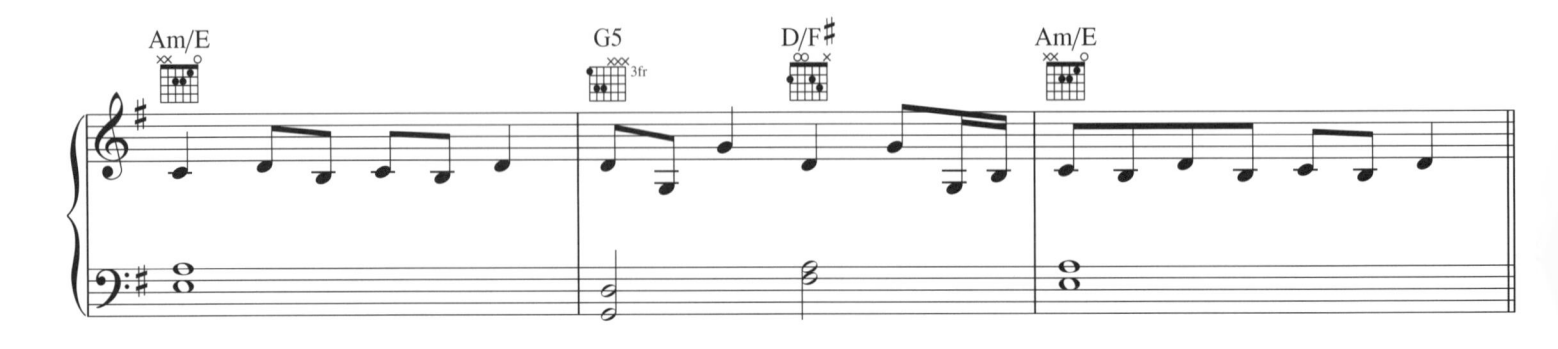

Gentle Ballad

You spoke_ and worlds_ were formed,_ You breathed_ and life_ was born._
You lived_ a sin - less life,___ yet You__ were cru - ci - fied._

You knew__ that one_ day You__ would come.
You bought_ our free - dom on__ the cross.

So far__ from Heav - en's throne,_ clothed_ in hu - man form,_
For - sak - en for__ our sin,___ You died and rose_ a - gain._

You showed_ the world_ the Fa - ther's love._
Je - sus,___ You are__ the Lamb_ of God._

You gave,_

G ... You gave Your life a-way. **D** You gave, You gave Your life a-way. You gave,

Em7 You gave Your life a-way for me. **C** Your grace

G has bro-ken ev-'ry chain, my sins are gone, **D** my debt's been paid. You gave,

Em7 You gave Your life a-way for me, **C** for

me.

me. How glo-rious is __ Your love. __ If I __ could sing for-ev-er, it's not e-nough. __ How glo-rious is __ Your love. __ If I __ could sing for-ev-er, it's not e-nough, ___ it's not e-nough. 'Cause You gave, ___ You gave __ Your life __ a-way. You gave, ___ You gave __ Your life __ a-way. You gave, ___ You gave __ Your life __ a-way for _____ me. Your grace ___ has bro-ken ev-'ry chain, my sins ___ are gone, __ my debt's __ been paid. You gave, __

303

Oh, thank You, Lord, oh, thank You, Lord.

For-sak-en for my sin, You died and rose a-gain.

Je-sus, You are the Lamb of God.

YOUR LOVE NEVER FAILS

Words and Music by ANTHONY SKINNER
and CHRIS McCLARNEY

sep - a - rate. E - ven if I ran a - way, Your __ love nev - er fails. __ Mm. __

I know I __ still make mis - takes, but You have new mer - cy for me ev - 'ry day, 'cause Your __ love nev - er fails. __

307

the oceans rage, I don't have to be afraid, because I know that You love me, and Your love never fails.

The wind is strong and the

wa-ter's deep, __ but I'm not a-lone here in these o-pen seas, __ 'cause Your __ love nev-er fails. __ Mm. __

The cha-sm __ was far too wide; __ I nev-er thought I'd reach the oth-er side, but Your __

F♯m7
Dsus2
A
love never fails. Thank You, Jesus, thank You, Jesus.
E
D.S. al Coda
Oh.
CODA
E
Dsus2
love, oh... And all things
F♯m7
Esus
E
Esus
E
work together for my good. Oh, Lord, oh, You make
Dsus2
F♯m7
1
Esus
E
all things work together for my good. Oh, You make,

311

oh, You make... __ good. You __ stay the same. Oh. __

Well, You stay the same __ through the ag - es.

Your __ love nev - er chang - es. __ There may be

pain in __ the night, but joy comes __ with the morn -

-ing. Oh, Lord. And when the oceans rage, I don't have to be afraid, be-cause I know that You love me, oh, You stay the same.

2
E
Esus
Dsus2
and Your love nev - er fails.
F♯m7
Esus
Your love nev - er fails, Your love nev - er fails.
mp
Dsus2
F♯m7
E
All things
all things
work to - geth - er for my good.
Repeat ad lib. and Fade
Optional Ending
A
Lord, You make
rit.

YOUR GREAT NAME

Words and Music by MICHAEL NEALE
and KRISSY NORDHOFF

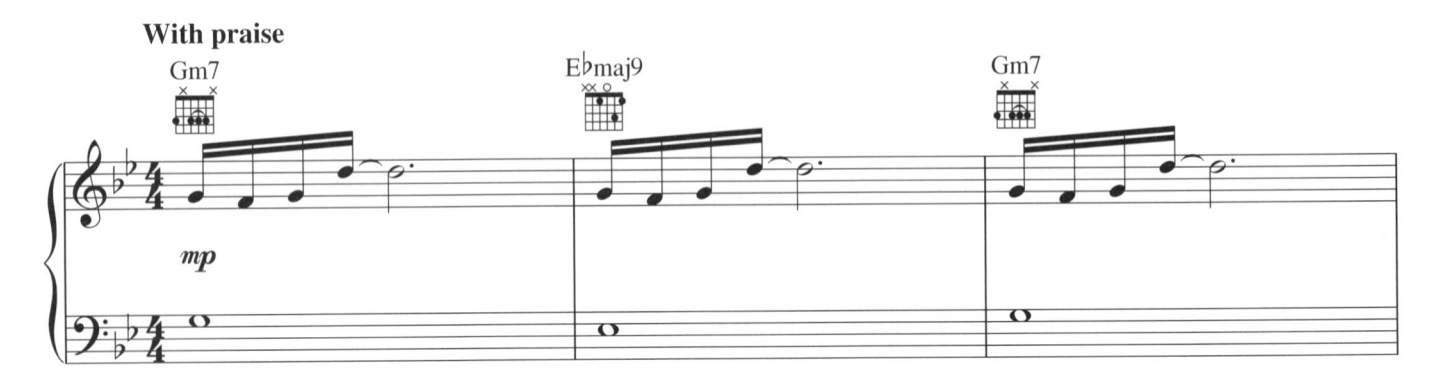

With praise

Lost are saved, find their way at the sound of Your great name. All con-demned feel no

© 2008 INTEGRITY'S PRAISE! MUSIC (BMI) and TWONORDS MUSIC (ASCAP)
INTEGRITY'S PRAISE! MUSIC Admin. at EMICMGPUBLISHING.COM
TWO NORDS MUSIC Admin. by MUSIC SERVICES
All Rights Reserved Used by Permission

shame at the sound of Your great name. Ev - 'ry

fear has no place at the sound of Your great

name. The en - e - my, he has to leave at the sound

of Your great name. Je - sus,

worthy is the Lamb that was slain for us, Son of God and man. You are high and lifted up, and all the world will praise Your great name.

All the weak find their strength at the sound of Your great

F
Gm
E♭/G
E♭
name. Hun - gry souls re - ceive grace at the sound
B♭
F/A
Gm
of Your great name. The fa - ther - less, they find their
E♭/G
E♭
B♭
Dm
rest at the sound of Your great name. The sick are healed
Gm
E♭/G
E♭
B♭
and the dead are raised at the sound of Your great

F Eb Bb F Gm
name. Je - sus, wor-thy is the Lamb that was
Eb Bb F Gm Eb Bb
slain for us, Son of God and man. You are high and lift-ed up, and
Gm F Eb Bb
all the world will praise Your great name,
F Eb Bb F
oh, Your great name.
3fr
f

Gm Eb Gm F Gm
Re - deem - er, my Heal - er, Lord Al - might - y, my Sav - ior, De - fend - er,
Eb Bb F Gm Eb Gm
You are my King. Re - deem - er, my Heal - er, Lord Al - might - y,
F Gm Eb Fsus F Eb Bb
my Sav - ior, De - fend - er, You are my King. Je - sus,
mp
F Gm Eb6 Bb F6 Gm
the name of Je - sus. You are

high and lift-ed up, ___ and all the world ___ will praise Your great

name. Je-sus, ___ wor-thy is ___ the Lamb ___ that was

slain for us, ___ Son of God ___ and man. ___ You are

high and lift-ed up, ___ and all the world ___ will praise Your great ___

E♭ B♭ F Dm E♭ Gm
name, Your great name,
F Dm E♭ Gm F
Your great name.
E♭ B♭ F Gm E♭ B♭
Je - sus. Je - sus.
mp
Repeat and Fade
Optional Ending
F Gm F Gm F E♭(add2)
rit.

YOUR NAME

Words and Music by PAUL BALOCHE and GLENN PACKIAM

*Recorded a half step lower.

© 2006 INTEGRITY'S HOSANNA! MUSIC (ASCAP) and VERTICAL WORSHIP SONGS (ASCAP)
Admin. at EMICMGPUBLISHING.COM
All Rights Reserved   Used by Permission

songs of praise __ that rise from earth __ to touch __ Your heart __ and glo-ri-fy __ Your name. __ Your name _____ is a strong and might-y tow-er. Your name _____ is a shel-ter like __ no oth-er. Your name, _____ let the nations sing it loud-er, 'cause noth-ing has the pow-er to save but Your name.

Je-sus, in Your name we pray, come and fill our

hearts to-day. Lord, give us strength to live for You and glo-ri-fy Your name. Your name but Your name.

'Cause Your name is a strong and mighty tower. Your name is a shelter like no other. Your name, let the nations sing it louder, 'cause nothing has the power to save. Your name is a strong and might-y tow-er. Your name is a shel-ter like no oth-er. Your name, let the na-tions sing it loud-er, 'cause noth-ing has the pow-er to save but Your name.

Csus2/E
Fsus2
G/B
Am7
Na na na na na na. Na na na na na na.
Csus2/E
Fsus2
G/B
Am7
Na na na na na na. Na na na na na na.
Csus2/E
Fsus2
G/B
Am7
mf
Csus2/E
Fsus2
G5
3fr
C5
3fr
rit.